A World of Tricksters

Richard Marsh

Legendary Books

Legendary Books
A World of Tricksters
ISBN: 978-0-915330-17-1

Published by

Richard Marsh
15 Fontenoy Street
Dublin 7, Ireland
Phone 353-1-8827941
www.RichardMarsh.ie
Richard@RichardMarsh.ie

Also by Richard Marsh:

Hellhounds and Hero Horses: Beasts of Myth and Legend,
    Legendary Books, 2020
Meath Folk Tales, The History Press Ireland, 2013
Irish King and Hero Tales, Legendary Books, 2011
Irische Königs- und Heldensagen, the German edition of
    Irish King and Hero Tales, Edition Narrenflug, 2014
Spanish and Basque Legends, Legendary Books, 2010
Tales of the Wicklow Hills, Legendary Books, 2007
The Legends and Lands of Ireland, Sterling, 2004

Front cover: Fiona Dowling – The Narrow-striped Kern.
See page 46.

Frontispiece: Sosruko Fetches Fire – detail from the coat
of arms of Adygea. See page 36.

Back cover: the bridge at Oiartzun, See page 69.

Richard Marsh is a storyteller in Ireland and other
countries and a Legendary Tour guide in Ireland, taking
people to the places where the stories happened.

He who desires to be well acquainted with a people will not reject their popular stories or local superstitions. Depend upon it, that man is too far advanced into an artificial state of society who is a stranger to the effects which tales and stories like these have upon the feelings of a nation; and his opinions of its character are never likely to be more erroneous than when, in the pride of reason, he despises such means of forming his judgment.
John Malcolm, *Sketches of Persia*, 1861

"Stories ain't never done no harm to nobody. And if they don't do no good, how come they last so long?"
Uncle Remus, from the Disney film *Song of the South*, 1946

Morality is not the issue in these tales, but rather, assurance that one can succeed.
Bruno Bettelheim, *The Uses of Enchantment: The Meaning and Importance of Fairy Tales*, 1976

The supreme art of war is to subdue the enemy without fighting.
Sun Tzu, *The Art of War*, fourth century BC

Riches – sin before God; poverty – sin before men.
Russian proverb

Richard Marsh's *A World of Tricksters* is a good romp through all the facets of the trickster motif, from mythology to urban legend.

With occasional reference to Stith-Thompson's index, Richard's sources range from Petronius' first century AD work, *Satyricon*, to his own personal recollections. Characters such as the mythical Native American Coyote to the twentieth century gambler Barney Curley fill the pages.

Think of this book as good bedtime reading. The stories are short and the laughs come quickly. Richard's observations and dry humor add to the book's enjoyment.

Charles Kiernan, American storyteller

A fantastic resource – chock full of great stories and essential, well-researched background material. Just what I need!

Jill Lamede, The Tintagel Storyteller, England

This book is a Storyteller's delight. Trickster tales from around the world supplemented with rich notes, discussion of sources and informative introductions make this an exhaustive encyclopaedia to include in the Storyteller's repertoire.

Professor Vinita Dhondiyal Bhatnagar
Rajiv Gandhi Technological University, Bhopal
Madhya Pradesh. India.

This book is a treasure trove of trickster stories from around the world and a great resource for teachers, tellers, and lovers of story.

MyLinda Butterworth, American storyteller and award-winning author of *The Monster Run*

Richard Marsh's wide knowledge of world folklore gives us a wonderful collection of tales of trickery. Every lover of storytelling should have this book.

Richard Martin, British storyteller, Germany, Amazon review

There can never be enough books about tricksters. Richard Marsh is one of the most meticulous researchers and most enthusiastic storytellers I know; kind of a trickster himself. He gathers some rare stories in this book, revealing the amazing diversity of trickster characters around the world, with a special focus on Irish trickery.

Tarkabarka, United States, Amazon review

Lost in another world, or rather worlds, I was taken away with Richard Marsh's latest. *A World of Tricksters* is like a nice bottle of whiskey to be savored one, or two, delicious tastes at a time. Or go ahead and binge a little! Either way, you'll find some familiar but mostly new stories of how cleverness and intelligence triumph.

In clear prose, *A World of Tricksters* gives us little known stories from several cultures, traditional to contemporary urban legends. As a long-time resident of America's north woodlands, I particularly enjoyed reading Ojibwe folktales alongside Asian, South American, African and European tales celebrating wit and intelligence.

Yvonne Healy, American storyteller
Member of Red Internacional de Cuentacuentos – International Storytelling Network

With wit and a somewhat twisted sense of humor, *A World of Tricksters* will delight you but at the same time make you wonder: who is the real trickster? Tricksters will make you laugh, they'll make you wonder. But be careful, for they may make even you stumble.

Professor María Alejandra Gómez de la Torre Barúa
(To whom I am grateful for pointing out an embarrassing typo.)
English teacher and storyteller, Peru
Member of Red Internacional de Cuentacuentos – International Storytelling Network

Contents

Humans

Irish Highwaymen, Tories and Rapparees 154

Latin American Tricksters

A Bag of Irish Tricks

Racing

Foreword

Bairbre Ní Fhloinn

From the exploits of Hermes in ancient Greece to those of Loki in Norse mythology, from the tales of Chaucer in medieval England to stories still told in Ireland about the great nineteenth-century statesman, Daniel O'Connell, the world, it would seem, loves a rogue. In the pages of this book, Richard Marsh presents a compelling selection of wayward geniuses, inventive intellects and "desperate underdogs", as he puts it, in a celebration of the figure of the trickster in popular tradition from China to North America, with many stop-overs in between. Smooth operators from the most diverse cultures rub shoulders with each other in illustration of the perennial appeal of this most fascinating of archetypes.

The figure of the trickster is a cultural universal which survives and thrives into the present, often telling us more about ourselves than about the characters in the stories. Ambivalence and ambiguity are the order of the day as the trickster emerges as hero and villain at one and the same time, providing a unique insight into the human psyche and into our deepest desires and fantasies. In terms of popular culture and tradition, the stories in this collection demonstrate the reality of globalization before the word was invented, as evidence that the trickster knows no boundaries, has no national allegiance and carries no passport.

As a genre, these stories are often highly subtle and sophisticated in the messages they carry and in the lessons they teach. Despite their undoubted entertainment value and ostensibly humorous nature, and as touched on by Richard Marsh in his insightful Introduction, many of them are characterised by an underlying philosophy touching on the most profound issues of human existence and personal morality. This is the "dead seriousness" which the renowned American folklorist Henry Glassie describes in his book, *The Stars of Ballymenone*, in his commentary on the story of Willie the Wisp, a tale commonly told in Ireland about a man who sells his soul to the devil – an international motif found in several of the stories in the present collection. In other words – and as in our dealings with any good trickster – we should never fall into the trap of underestimating this material and what it has to offer us.

With this book, Richard Marsh has performed a great service to everyone interested in traditional oral narrative in all its richness and complexity. He has journeyed through many cultures in his search for the trickster, providing illuminating background material and fascinating snippets of information along the way. Throughout the work, he highlights the connections and parallels which exist between trickster narratives from ancient times and similar anecdotes in circulation today, thus making the material all the more immediate and meaningful. The World of Tricksters unveiled in these pages is at once exotic and familiar, universal and local, entertaining and profound. For bringing together these chancers, rogues and heroes and introducing them to us, we owe Richard Marsh a debt of gratitude.

Dr Bairbre Ní Fhloinn lectures in Irish Folklore and Ethnology in the UCD School of Irish, Celtic Studies and Folklore. She is Director of the recently established MA in Irish Folklore and Ethnology, which she initiated.

Introduction

The Purpose of Trickster Tales

Folk tales are both conservative and subversive – supporting the ethos of a society and subverting the status quo when it is unjust. Subversion often comes in the form of a trick, which is an action taken for the real (and ideally legitimate, though perhaps illegal) benefit of the trickster or another person against the unjust behaviour of those with the advantage of class, wealth, authority or physical superiority. That benefit can be material – the saving of life, avoiding injury or capture, economic survival – or the preservation of dignity and a positive self-image through mockery or humiliation as a form of psychological revenge: taking the high and mighty down a peg or two. Like modern political cartoons.

Stories about tricks are entertaining, but they carry a serious message for the young, weak, vulnerable, and socially disadvantaged: it is possible to overcome bullying, whether institutional or personal, or at least counter its effects.

This lesson is encoded in narratives for a good reason: "There are some areas of the mind which can only be reached with stories, because they penetrate deep into the subconscious, like ink dripped on to blotting paper" (Idries Shah). John Ruskin referred to the humanizing power of traditional tales "to fortify children against the glacial cold of science". We might add "negative elements in society". The collector Antonio de Trueba commented: "In the folk tale is found everything that can be found in literature: morals, science, arts, history, customs, philosophy – in a word, everything that human knowledge embraces."

Pranks, including hoaxes and practical jokes, fail to meet the criteria of tricks on three counts: the perpetrators are not underdogs; they derive no real and legitimate benefit from the prank; and the underlying purpose of a prank is humour – often cruel – and the usually undeserved embarrassment of the victim. Examples in the Pranks section illustrate the difference.

This representative but far from comprehensive collection includes historical personages from the fourth-century BC Chinese philosopher Chwang Tze to the tenth-century Saint Olga of Russia to the 21st-century Irish gambler Barney Curley, as well as demi-gods who help the Creator (and themselves), animals derived from those culture heroes, and a global cross-section of desperate underdogs struggling to survive in adverse conditions.

The Divine Origin of the Trickster

All cultures recognize a supreme being who created the world. Usually there are helper beings who then refined creation: separated land and water, supplied vegetation, formed or improved humans and other animals, and taught the humans arts and crafts. The Native American trickster Coyote stole fire from the Fire Beings and showed humans how to use it. Christianity saw some of these demi-gods as supernatural competitors in league with Satan and condemned them as enemies of God. Others were replaced with angels and saints: Saint Eustace, one of the Fourteen Holy Helpers, took over as a patron of hunters from the panoply of pagan deities; San Martín Txiki tricked secrets of agriculture out of the giant basajauns and shared them with the Basques.

Those left out of that dichotomy of good and evil serve as benevolent pre-Christian versions of the Holy Helpers and can be found in fairy tales in the form of a little old man encountered along the path or a little old woman in a cottage. These are testers and teachers of tricks, stripped of divine characteristics but retaining magic powers and preternatural wisdom and knowledge, who set difficult tasks for the hero or heroine in order to help them fulfil their potential.

The archetypal trickster is a part god-like and part human-like creature, usually in male form, who exists between this world and the Otherworld. He is a messenger between humans and the divine sphere, like the Roman god Mercury and his Greek counterpart, Hermes. These trickster demi-gods are current in many cultures, including Native American myth (Manabozho, Coyote), Anansi and Kalulu folk tales in Africa, and Irish literature and storytelling (Manannán mac Lir as the Narrow-striped Kern, for example).

Scholarly comments on a Brazilian demi-god throw light on the trickster character in general. Exú (pronounced "eh-SHOO") is an Orixá ("oh-ree-SHAH") imported by African slaves in the 16th century, blended with native personages, and still active in current Candomblé and capoeira practices. These are snippets from an article by Floyd Merrell on the now defunct Trickster's Way website.

"Exu is the quintessential rebel against customs, conventions, and norms. ... is conformity and resistance ... he is the eternal intermediary between men and women and the gods ... a mediator and messenger interacting between the Orixás and worldly beings. He is who helps make Axé [the life-force] happen. ... he existed before all the other Orixás; he existed before the world order. In fact, he is of the nature of life itself. ... he is the projection of the Africans' longing for freedom ... He creates an enigmatic union between the Sacred and the Profane, Culture and Nature, Civilization and Barbarism."

In his book *Exu: Trickster by Default* (2003), Merrell says: "Candomblé consisted in an outward show of conformity with the wishes of the masters while concealing an undercurrent of hidden resilience that often exploded into open resistance, a combination of physical and emotional survival. To call Exu a god-like trickster is a gross over-simplification of his role in Candomblé, but it will have to do for the purposes of this book."

The spirit of Exú lives not far beneath the surface of the characters in the following stories.

Native American myths and the Nart tales come first in the text, because they clearly portray the trickster as demi-

14

god, followed by the roughly corresponding Irish god-figures Gobán Saor and Manannán mac Lir, and then the Ultimate Trickster and demonized demi-god, the Devil. Next are folk tales of animals, who are the nearest descendants of the demi-gods. The rest of the stories are about humans, more or less timeless and in no particular order, followed by "Pranks" and the do-it-yourself "Bones" compilation.

Some entries are followed by a tag, such as "J1172. Judgment as rebuke to unjust plaintiff" in the "Daniel O'Connell" chapter. The number and description come from Stith Thompson's *Motif-Index of Traditional Folk-Literature*, Bloomington: Indiana University Press, 1955, 6 vols. Also online.

You may notice that Ireland is well represented here. After seven centuries of domination by a foreign power, retaliation is often applauded, especially if the victim of the mischief is British. A perfect example of this is "The Train in the Tunnel". The Irish love a scamp.

Native American Trickster Gods

These trickster gods are archetypes or demi-gods in human form with shape-shifting and other magic powers and exaggerated attributes of the animals whose names they bear: Coyote, Spider and White Hare, who is known as Manabozho among the Ojibwe. Collectively they are called the First People, or simply the People, as distinguished from humans (New People, or "people" with a small "p") and animals. They typically recognize an omnipotent Creator, who they assist in creating humans and natural features, and they sometimes become natural features such as Sun and Moon. A combination of benevolent and malicious, kind and selfish, they trick and test and teach humans and animals, and are often tricked and defeated and made to look foolish by their intended victims.

Although "manidoo" and its variants are neutral words meaning "spirit" or "god", the term is often used for those of the People who are completely wicked – enemies of the People and humans alike. It is part of the responsibility of the tricksters, in preparing the world for human inhabitants, to destroy them.

Manabozho
Ojibwe (Ojibway, Chippewa) – Algonquian Language Group
Canada and the United States: Great Lakes Region

Henry Wadsworth Longfellow tells the story of Manabozho in his 1855 epic poem, *The Song of Hiawatha*, based on traditional Algonquian stories collected by Henry Rowe Schoolcraft with the help of his bilingual Scots-Irish-Ojibwe wife, Jane Johnston. The Ojibwe trickster god Manabozho is known to the Iroquois as Hiawatha. Some commentators feel that he has been conflated with the historical Mohawk named Hiawatha, who united five squabbling nations to form the Iroquois Confederacy in the 16th century. In his 1856 collection *The Myth of Hiawatha*, Schoolcraft complains that no publisher in the United States or Europe was interested in the 1839 version of his book, and he credits Longfellow with bringing the stories to public attention: "... had it not been for the attractive poetic form in which one of our most popular and successful bards has clothed some of these wild myths, the period of their reproduction is likely to have been still further postponed. ... Mr. Longfellow has given prominence to [the myth of Manabozho], and to its chief episodes, by selecting and generalizing such traits as appeared best susceptible of poetic uses."

Manabozho helped Gitchi-manidoo (Great Spirit) create the world. As a boy, he lived on the shore of Gitchigami (Big Lake: Lake Superior) with his grandmother, Nokomis (Grandmother: the Earth Mother), daughter of the moon. Pregnant by her husband, Nokomis had been ejected from the moon by a love rival and landed on the earth, where she gave birth to a daughter, Wenonah, Manabozho's mother. Wenonah died when Manabozho was born. Nokomis taught Manabozho the language of the birds and animals and all their secrets.

One day Manabozho asked her if he had any other relatives.

"Your father is Ningabiun, the West Wind, whose cruelty killed your mother when you were born. Your brothers are Kabibonokka the North Wind, Wabun the East Wind and Shawondasee the South Wind."

(Ningabiun is called Mudjekeewis in *The Song of Hiawatha*.)

Manabozho travelled west with the intention of killing his father to avenge his mother's death. They fought to a draw, and Ningabiun told him to use his powers to help humans by teaching them and by killing monsters that harassed them.

One day, he decided to kill Pearl Feather (Megissogwon), the shining manidoo who had killed Nokomis' husband when he came to earth from the moon

17

to rescue her. The manidoo's lodge was on the far side of Gitchigami and was protected by serpents that belched fire constantly across a narrow pass, and then by a lake of pitch that would stop any boat that managed to escape the serpents. Manabozho loaded his canoe with his bow and arrows and a plentiful supply of oil, which he had taken from a king fish he had just killed. He only had to speak his destination and the canoe would take him there.

When he arrived at the serpents, he approached as close as he could while staying outside the range of their flames. He greeted them in a friendly manner, but they said, "We know you, Manabozho, and we won't let you pass."

He turned as if to retreat, but then pointed behind the serpents and shouted, "What's that?"

When they turned to look, he spoke to his canoe and glided quickly past them, then shot them all with his arrows. He came to the lake of pitch and rubbed the fish oil all over the canoe, which slipped easily through the sticky mass, and he landed in sight of Pearl Feather's lodge.

"Attack! Run! Surround him!" he shouted in different voices to make the manidoo think there were many attackers. Pearl Feather came out of his lodge and began to shower him with arrows. Manabozho dodged and fired back, shooting all but three of his arrows. Then a woodpecker flew to him and said, "Shoot at the lock of hair on the crown of his head. That's his vulnerable spot."

Manabozho aimed one arrow at the spot and wounded the manidoo, the second brought him to his knees, and the third killed him. Manabozho dipped his hand in the manidoo's blood and smeared it on the woodpecker's head, and that is why the woodpecker's head is red to this day.

Manabozho helped make the world safe for the People and the New People – humans – but he also played tricks on the animals.

He captured a fish of such monstrous size, that the fat and oil he obtained from it formed a small lake. He therefore invited all the animals and fowls to a banquet, and he made the order in which they partook of this repast the measure of their fatness. As fast as they arrived, he told them to plunge in. The bear came first, and was followed by the deer, opossum, and such other animals as are noted for their peculiar fatness at certain seasons. The moose and bison came tardily. The partridge looked on till the reservoir was nearly exhausted. The hare and marten came last, and these animals have, consequently, no fat.

When this ceremony was over, he told the assembled animals and birds to dance, taking up his drum and crying, "New songs from the south, come, brothers, dance." He directed them to pass in a circle around him, and to shut their eyes. They did so. When he saw a fat fowl pass by him, he adroitly wrung off its head, at the same time beating his drum and singing with greater vehemence, to drown the noise of the fluttering, and crying out, in a tone of admiration, "That's the way, my brothers, *that's* the way."

At last a small duck (the diver), thinking there was something wrong, opened one eye and saw what he was doing. Giving a spring, and crying, "Ha-ha-a! Manabozho is killing us," he made for the water. Manabozho followed him, and, just as the duck was getting into the water, gave him a kick, which is the cause of his back being flattened and his legs being straightened out backward, so that when he gets on land he cannot walk, and his tail feathers are few. Meantime the other birds flew off, and the animals ran into the woods.

(From *The Myth of Hiawatha*)

(Lame Deer tells that story with Iktome the Spider as the hero in his book *Lame Deer: Seeker of Visions*.)

19

Manabozho took the birds he had killed and proceeded to roast them in a sand oven. He buried them in the sand, some with their heads sticking up and others with their legs sticking up, and gathered wood and built a fire over them to slow-cook them. This would take a long time, and he was tired from all the singing and music-making and dancing, so he lay down for a nap. While he was asleep, a group of Winnebagos arrived in their canoes and saw an opportunity for a free feast. They pulled out all the birds, which were well cooked by then. They ate till they were full and took the remains with them when they left, replacing the heads and feet where they had found them. Manabozho went hungry that day.

He was walking along the shore of Lake Saint Clair, between Michigan and Ontario, when he saw some ducks and geese on the water and thought he'd try that trick again. He took out his drum and beat it and sang, "New songs. I am bringing new songs."

When the ducks came close to the shore, he challenged them to a diving competition. They accepted, and he beat them. Then he challenged the geese. He dived under them and tied their legs together with cord made from basswood bark. When the geese realized what he was doing, they all flew up, dragging Manabozho with them, as he was hanging on to the cord. They flew higher and higher until the cord broke, and Manabozho fell to the ground.

Dais-Imid (He of the Little Shell)
Ojibwe (Ojibway, Chippewa) – Algonquian Language Group
Canada and the United States: Great Lakes Region

Manabozho frequently didn't have things his own way. There was a man named Dais-Imid, He of the Little Shell, for the magic shell that his sister had hung around his neck. He never grew beyond the size of an infant, though he became a mighty hunter. One day he came across Manabozho killing beavers from the beaver lodge that

20

Dais-Imid and his sister owned. As Manabozho was taking them away on a sled, Dais-Imid cut off the tail of one of them and took it home. Manabozho noticed that one tail was missing and wondered about it. The following two days the same thing happened, and Manabozho was perplexed, because Dais-Imid had made himself invisible, and he was so light-footed that he left no tracks in the snow.

On the third day Dais-Imid decided to let Manabozho see him.

"I'm going to kill you," said Manabozho.

"You can't."

Manabozho grabbed at him, but Dais-Imid disappeared.

"Where are you?"

"I'm inside your belt."

Manabozho punched and pounded at his belt, but the little man was gone again, and Manabozho got nothing but bruises for his trouble.

"Where are you now?"

"I'm in your right nostril."

Manabozho tweaked and pinched his nose as hard as he could, but the voice came from the ground: "Now I'm here."

He made himself visible and said, "I've taken another beaver tail for my sister. Goodbye, Manabozho." And he strode away with a gleaming light around his head.

When the time came for Dais-Imid and his sister to part, she chose to live in the east, "the place of the breaking of daylight", where she became the Morning Star.

"And I," said he, "my sister, shall live on the mountains and rocks. There I can see you at the earliest hour, and there the streams of water are clear, and the air pure. And I shall ever be called Puck Wudj Ininee, or the little wild man of the mountains." (*The Myth of Hiawatha*)

A tribe of these Puk Wudj Ininees – "fairies" in English – are called Mish-in-e-mok-in-ok-ong, or turtle spirits, and are said to inhabit Michilimackinac –

Mackinac Island – located between the Upper and Lower Peninsulas of Michigan. Alternatively, they are descendants of the survivors of a massacre by Senecas of Mish-in-e-mok-in-ok-ong who fled to the forest and are now supernatural beings called Bgoji-nishnaabensag, which means "little people".

> *Mishinimakinago; pl.-g.*—This name is given to some strange Indians (according to the sayings of the Otchipwes [Ojibwe]), who are rowing through the woods, and who are sometimes heard shooting, but never seen. And from this word, the name of the village of *Mackinac*, or *Michillimackinac*, is derived.

(Baraga, *A Dictionary of the Otchipwe Language.* "Rowing" and "shooting" are thus in the dictionary, but "roving" and "shouting" seem more likely.)

Paup-Puk-Keewiss (Grasshopper)
Ojibwe (Ojibway, Chippewa) – Algonquian Language Group
Canada and the United States: Great Lakes Region

Dais-Imid had a cousin named Paup-Puk-Keewiss (Grasshopper), who was a small man, though not tiny like Dais-Imid, but possessed of prodigious strength. His lodge was near the shore of Gitchigami, but he liked to travel in search of adventure. One day, when he came to a village, the people giggled when he told them his name, but they invited him to share a meal. Unfortunately, he couldn't control his strength. Even if he tried to set a plate down gently, it broke. If he shook hands with a man he tore his arm off. If he stretched, he lifted the roof off the lodge. When he gave a playful push to a boy and sent him flying out of sight never to be found, he was asked to leave. A young man who had taken a liking to him went with him and served as his pipe-bearer. Paup-Puk-Keewiss was a big smoker. When people saw a cloud of smoke in the distance, they would say, "Here comes Paup-Puk-Keewiss."

He arrived at another village, where they told him that fierce cannibal manidoos were eating the people. Paup-Puk-Keewiss said he would look into the problem. The chief offered to send twenty warriors to help, but Paup-Puk-Keewiss said they wouldn't be necessary. The chief sent them anyway. The pipe-bearer grinned, for he knew his master's strength. When they arrived at the manidoos' lodge, Paup-Puk-Keewiss told his companions to stay back and watch.

He went into the lodge and saw five manidoos, a father and his four sons. They glared at him with eyes set low in their faces, munching and slobbering over pieces of meat as if they were starving. They offered him a piece, but it looked like a human thigh and he declined.

"What do you want?" one said.

"Nothing. Where is your uncle?"

"We ate him yesterday. What do you want?"

"Nothing. Where is your grandfather?"

"We ate him last week. Do you want to wrestle?"

"I don't mind, if you go easy on me. As you can see, I'm much smaller than you."

"Pity he's so small and thin," one of them said to the others.

"The closer to the bone, the sweeter the meat," said another with a wicked roll of his eyes.

"You go first," said the father to the oldest son.

They went outside, and Paup-Puk-Keewiss and the manidoo grappled and threw each other around. Just as the manidoo was trying to bite Paup-Puk-Keewiss on the shoulder, he tripped up the manidoo and aimed his head toward a rock, killing him. He sent the next two flying in different directions, and the fourth he threw straight up in the air never to be seen again in this world.

The father took to his heels. For a time, Paup-Puk-Keewiss toyed with him, chasing behind, running next to him, then in front of him, while the old one huffed and puffed. When he got bored with the game, he gave the manidoo a kick that sent him tumbling through the air until he landed on the back of a bull buffalo. The buffalo set off at a gallop, and that was the last anyone ever heard of that manidoo.

Paup-Puk-Keewiss was a crazy brain, who played many queer tricks, but took care, nevertheless, to supply his family and children with food. But in this he was not always successful. Many winters have passed since he was overtaken, at this very season of the year, with great want, and he, with his whole family, was on the point of starvation. Every resource seemed to have failed. The snow was so deep, and the storm continued so long, that he could not even find a partridge or a hare. And his usual resource of fish had entirely failed. His lodge stood in a point of woods, not far back from the shores of the Gitchigami, or great water, where the autumnal storms had piled up the ice into high pinnacles, resembling castles.

"I will go," said he to his family one morning, "to these castles, and solicit the pity of the spirits who inhabit them, for I know that they are the residence of some of the spirits of Kabiboonoka." He did so, and found that his petition was not disregarded. They told him to fill his mushkemoot, or sack, with the ice and snow, and pass on toward his lodge, without looking back, until he came to a certain hill. He must then drop it and leave it till morning, when he would find it filled with fish.

They cautioned him, that he must by no means look back, although he would hear a great many voices crying out to him, in abusive terms, for these voices were nothing but the wind playing through the branches of the trees. He faithfully obeyed the injunction, although he found it hard to avoid turning round, to see who was calling out to him. And when he visited his sack in the morning, he found it filled with fish.

24

It chanced that Manabozho visited him on the morning that he brought home the sack of fish. He was invited to partake of a feast, which Paup-Puk-Keewiss ordered to be prepared for him. While they were eating, Manabozho could not help asking him, by what means he had procured such an abundance of food, at a time when they were all in a state of starvation.

Paup-Puk-Keewiss frankly told him the secret, and repeated the precautions which were necessary to insure success. Manabozho determined to profit by his information, and as soon as he could, he set out to visit the icy castles. All things happened as he had been told. The spirits seemed propitious, and told him to fill and carry. He accordingly filled his sacks with ice and snow, and proceeded rapidly toward the hill of transmutation. But as he ran he heard voices calling out behind him, "Thief! thief! He has stolen fish from Kabiboonoka," cried one. "Mukumik! mukumik! Take it away! Take it away!" cried another.

In fine, his ears were so assailed by all manner of opprobrious terms, that he could not avoid turning his head to see who it was that thus abused him. But his curiosity dissolved the charm. When he came to visit his bags next morning, he found them filled with ice and snow.

(From *The Myth of Hiawatha*)

A giant manidoo who was Manabozho's cousin had heard of the trick Dais-Imid had played on Manabozho with the beaver tails, and to avenge the insult to Manabozho he caught the little fellow and threw him into a large kettle which he kept on the boil. With his magic shell, Dais-Imid bailed out all the water and escaped. Paup-Puk-Keewiss decided to take revenge on Manabozho for the manidoo's attack on Dais-Imid, so he went to Manabozho's lodge when he was away and killed the birds that had come to visit, for Manabozho was their master and protector. Some birds escaped and reported the slaughter to Manabozho. He came quickly and started to chase Paup-Puk-Keewiss.

It was incumbent on Manabozho as the protector of nature to repair any damage done by Paup-Puk-Keewiss, and Paup-Puk-Keewiss knew this, so as he fled he stripped trees of their branches and shattered a rock so that Manabozho would be delayed by putting them right again. Finally he arrived at the foot of a cliff and saw a door. To his surprise, the manidoo who lived there opened the door and invited him in to his cave. No sooner had he entered than Manabozho came and pounded on the door.

"Open up!"

The manidoo said to Paup-Puk-Keewiss, "Since I have accepted you as my guest, I would rather die than open the door."

Hearing no reply, Manabozho said, "All right, Paup-Puk-Keewiss, you have until morning to live."

Paup-Puk-Keewiss thought his life was over, but the manidoo cheered him up.

"You have lived a foolish life," he said.

"I know."

"You have great gifts of strength."

"That's true."

"Yet you do nothing with these gifts but destroy things and hurt people."

"Mostly, yes."

"You should use your gifts for the benefit of humans."

"I see that now. My heart is changed. I will be good from now on."

When the morning came, Manabozho, sitting on a hill watching the manidoo's doorway, felt his strength diminish. Part of his power had gone, because he no longer had to contend with Paup-Puk-Keewiss's wicked ways. Paup-Puk-Keewiss was as good as his word, and he helped the People and humans.

In another version of the story, Manabozho destroyed the cave and killed the manidoo and Paup-Puk-Keewiss. He said to the spirit of Paup-Puk-Keewiss, "You shall not be again permitted to live on the earth. I will give you the

shape of the war-eagle, and you will be the chief of all
fowls, and your duty shall be to watch over their
destinies."

Raccoon and the Blind Men
United States: Menominee – Algonquian Language Group

Their village was vulnerable to attack, so the people
took two old blind men to the far side of the lake for
safety. They built a wigwam near the shore and stretched a
rope from the door of the wigwam to a pole set in the lake
near the shore so the men could find their way to water.
The villagers left food and dishes and other supplies and
promised they would bring provisions regularly.

The men were well able to look after themselves. They
shared chores: one day one would fetch water while the
other cooked, and the next day they would trade jobs.
They put enough food for both into one bowl, and both ate
out of it.

One day Raccoon was walking along the shore
searching for food and noticed the rope attached to the
pole. Curious, he followed the rope to the wigwam and
saw the two men sleeping. He smelled food but was afraid
he might wake the men, so he moved away from the
wigwam and watched.

The men awoke, and one said, "I'll go to the lake and
get some water while you cook the meal."

Raccoon saw him walk hand over hand along the rope
and realized he was blind. Raccoon scampered to the pole
and untied the rope and tied it to a clump of bushes. When
the man reached the bushes he was confused. He returned
to the wigwam and said, "The lake has dried up, and there
are bushes growing in it."

"That's impossible," said the other. "Even if the lake
dried overnight, there wouldn't be time for bushes to
grow. I'll go and try."

Raccoon untied the rope from the bushes and retied it
to the pole. The man followed the rope and filled his

bucket with water. When he returned to the wigwam, he said, "You were mistaken. The lake is full, and I have brought water."

The other man was even more puzzled. He cooked eight pieces of meat and put them in the bowl and placed it between them. The men each took one piece of meat and began to chew. Raccoon sneaked in and took four pieces and sat in the doorway eating and watching to see what would happen. When one man finished eating his piece, he put his hand in the bowl for another and said, "There are only two pieces left. You must have been very hungry to eat five pieces."

"I ate only one piece. You must have eaten the others."

They began to argue. Raccoon was enjoying the game, but to make it more fun he slapped both men on the cheek. Each thought the other had slapped him, and they began to fight, rolling over the floor scattering the fire. Raccoon laughed out loud, and the men realized they had been tricked. Raccoon grabbed the two remaining pieces of meat and ran off, calling over his shoulder, "You shouldn't be so quick to find fault."

K1081.2. Blind men duped into fighting: stolen meat. The trickster steals one piece of meat. The blind accuse each other and fight.

How Coyote Stole Fire
Central and Western United States

Coyote had no need for fire. His fur coat kept him warm in winter, and he liked his meat raw. But one spring day he was passing by a village and heard the women singing a song of mourning for the babies and old people who had died of the cold during the winter. It was his responsibility to help and teach the humans, and he saw that he had been neglecting his duty.

He shifted his form to that of an ordinary coyote and went to the mountain top where the three Fire Beings lived, jealously guarding fire so that humans couldn't use it and become as powerful as them. The Fire Beings sensed his presence and peered around them with their bloodstone eyes. One spotted him and said, "It's nothing, only a coyote hunting for food."

Coyote watched all day and all night. He saw how they worked in shifts: one guarded the fire and fed it dry branches and pine cones while the other two stayed in the tipi. He noticed that the fire was never left alone while the shifts changed – one came out of the tipi as the other went in – except at dawn. When the night watch Fire Being went into the tipi to wake up her replacement, there was a delay before she came out yawning and stretching – time enough for Coyote to steal the fire and get away with it. But he would need a bit of help.

He called a meeting with the rest of the People. He explained the problem of the furless humans and how he wanted to bring fire to them so they wouldn't suffer and die in the cold weather. The People all agreed to cooperate.

Coyote went back to the top of the mountain and lurked in the bushes. The Fire Beings noticed him and again dismissed him as just another coyote hunting. He waited until morning, when the sleepy Fire Being was slow to emerge from the tipi. The minute he saw that the fire was unguarded, Coyote leapt from the bushes and grabbed a glowing stick and started to run down the mountain with it. But as the Fire Being stumbled out of the tipi, she saw the glow moving away in the dim light and raised the alarm.

As fast as Coyote ran, the Fire Beings soon caught up with him. Just as one grabbed the tip of his tail, leaving a white mark which you see on coyotes today, he tossed the stick to Squirrel, who put it on her back and scampered through the treetops. The fire scorched her, curling her tail up over her back, the way it's been ever since. The Fire Beings now chased Squirrel until she tossed the burning stick to Chipmunk, who froze with fright. They pounced on Chipmunk and clawed at her back, leaving three stripes, before she darted away and threw the stick to Frog.

One of the Fire Beings grabbed his tail, pulling it off, but he managed to give the fire to Wood, who swallowed it.

The Fire Beings were flummoxed. They begged and pleaded with Wood to give the fire back to them. They sang and shouted and promised rewards, but Wood refused to surrender it, so eventually they went away.

Coyote, however, knew how to get fire out of Wood, and he taught the humans to rub sticks together and use a bowstring to spin a stick in a piece of Wood to entice fire out of it, and so the humans no longer had to suffer and die from the cold.

(Retold from Robinson, *Coyote the Trickster*.)

A1415. Theft of fire. Mankind is without fire. A culture hero steals it from owner.

A1415.2. Theft of fire by animals.

Coyote Tricked by Mice
United States

It had been a long hot day of walking, and at sundown Coyote found a cosy depression in the rocks just the right size for a bed. But he was kept awake by the mosquitoes that buzzed around his ears until the cool of the night drove them away, and then he was cold. He wrapped his tail around him and was just dozing off when he discovered that his bed was in the path of a horde of mice. They refused to take a detour and crawled and trotted over him. Half asleep, he tossed and turned and thrashed as the tiny feet trampled across his body.

Then the traffic stopped and it was quiet. Coyote slept briefly. Then the wailing began – high-pitched keening penetrating little voices that forced him to sit up and look around in the dawn light to see what was causing the commotion. Bodies of dead mice surrounded him, killed by his half-conscious thrashing and rolling. The mice were mourning and staring accusingly at him. He felt a little bit guilty, but, being Coyote, he quickly went on the defensive.

"It's all their own fault. If they had marched around me instead of using me as a shortcut, this would never have happened. Now go away and let me sleep."

The mice quietened and Coyote slept. Suddenly, with the sun fully risen, mouse voices woke him up with the universally recognized alarm call: danger is close!

"What is it? What's happening?" he said, springing to his feet.

"Hail storm! Big killer stones of ice! Anyone they hit will be dead!"

"You mice can hide in your burrows, but what can I do?"

"Not all of us can fit in the burrows at one time, so some of us hide in leather bags hung in the trees," they chattered hysterically.

"Do you have a bag big enough to fit me?"

"Just this one."

They showed him a bag of tough buffalo hide with a leather drawstring at the opening and a long rope slung over a tree limb.

"Quick, Coyote, get into the bag, and we'll haul you up into the tree where you'll be safe from the hail stones."

He climbed into the bag and drew the string closed. He felt himself being pulled up, then swaying in the breeze.

"There, Coyote. You're safe now. Here comes the hail."

He could feel the pattering of stones against the sides of the bag. Then the stones got bigger and sharper.

"Ooh, ow, ay!" he cried, as the stones rammed against his body through the buffalo hide. The storm grew in intensity, and all he could hear was the thud of bigger and bigger stones that bruised him all over. But he was grateful for the protection of the bag and the helpfulness of the mice, even though he had killed so many of them. Now he felt guilty.

Meanwhile, some of the People happened to be strolling nearby in the bright sunshine under a windless clear sky. They heard the cries of pain and recognized the voice as Coyote's. They came to investigate and saw a crowd of mice hurling stones at a leather bag strung in a tree. The shouts were coming from the bag as it squirmed and swung and bounced. A heap of sharp stones had collected under the bag. The People watched the mice pass larger and larger stones to those closest to the bag, who continued to pelt it unmercifully.

Quail, one of the People, said, "You are going to kill Coyote. Why are you doing this?"

The mice showed her the dead mice and explained how Coyote had killed them.

"They're dead because of Coyote's carelessness and selfishness. We won't kill him, because if we do he won't be alive to learn his lesson about considering others."

The cries from the bag had got weaker, and the mice lowered it and loosened the drawstring. When Coyote came out, blinking in the bright sunshine through swollen eyes, he saw the stones heaped under the bag instead of hail, and the mice and the People standing around staring at him, and instantly understood what had happened.

"You tricked me," he said to the mice, and that admission from the Master Trickster was worth more to the mice than an apology.

Q597. Animals avenge injury.

K713.1.1. Animal allows himself to be tied so as to avoid being carried off by storm.

Why Mount Shasta Erupted
Shasta Tribe
United States: Northern California and Southern Oregon

Mount Shasta, at the northern end of the Central Valley of California, is the second highest peak in the Cascade Range at 14,163 feet (4,317m). Its first eruption was 10,000 years ago, the most recent was in 1786, and it is considered an active volcano. Local myth tells of a battle between the sky god Skell, on the peak of Mount Shasta, and the underworld god Llao, on Mount Mazama in Oregon, in which they hurled boulders at each other.

Mazama was destroyed by an eruption about 5600 BC, and the collapsed remains form Crater Lake, the deepest lake in the United States at 1,949 feet (594m).

The Shasta people tell how Mount Shasta first erupted, and Coyote was involved.

Coyote, who was always hungry, found himself one spring day with nothing to eat, so he went to see the nearby Shastas. He knew that the Shastas were expert salmon fishermen and that the salmon were now running. Their culture demanded that they generously share their natural bounty: they were obliged by tradition to give as much as he could carry to anyone who asked for fish. So when Coyote arrived at a weir on one of the streams feeding the Klamath River and told the men he was hungry, they invited him to help himself.

But Coyote was so greedy he filled a huge sack with more fish than he could ever eat. As he carried the fish away, even with his great strength he had to stop and rest after a few miles. He lay face down on the earth with his sack still on his back and slept. While he was asleep, a swarm of yellow jackets came and devoured all the salmon, leaving only the bones. (Adult yellow jacket workers eat meat and fish and masticate it and take it back to the nest to feed to the larvae.)

When he awoke, Coyote was ravenous, and he thrust his face into the sack and took a mouthful – and spat out the bones in disgust. He searched all around and found no tracks of the thieves. Puzzled, he returned to the Shastas and told them that he had been robbed of the fish, and please could he have some more. They were happy to let him refill his sack.

Again he got tired on his way home and lay down for a rest in the same place, but this time he stayed awake to watch for the thieves. He noticed a swarm of yellow jackets approaching but didn't see them as a threat, so he took no action. But again, before he could stop them, they stripped all the flesh off the bones of the salmon. He returned again to the Shastas and explained what had happened. They gave him a third sack of fish and followed him. He sat down to rest, and the Shastas hid in the surrounding bushes. As they waited, Grandfather Turtle came strolling along and sat down near Coyote.

"Go away, Grandfather," said Coyote. "The Shastas and I are waiting for the yellow jackets that stole two sacks of salmon to try to steal this one so we can catch them at it."

But Grandfather Turtle ignored him and just sat there.

"You're in the way here, Grandfather. Move. You'll scare them off."

There was still no reaction from Grandfather Turtle. He was huge, much bigger than even the tortoises you see nowadays. Coyote glowered at him, knowing there was nothing he could do to get rid of him. While he was occupied doing this, the yellow jackets swooped in and stripped the salmon to the bones and flew away before Coyote or the Shastas could stop them. Recovering from their surprise, they took off hot-foot after them, but were soon outdistanced by the winged thieves. Grandfather Turtle set off in slow pursuit. Coyote and the Shastas soon tired of running and lay down to rest. Grandfather Turtle plodded patiently past them. He knew where the yellow jackets were heading, and he kept on a straight line for Mount Shasta.

He saw them pour in through a hole on top of the mountain with the stolen salmon. Although he was slow, he *was* big, and he took big, if ponderous, footsteps. By the time Coyote and the Shastas had recovered their energy and ran to catch up with him, he was already lumbering up the side of Mount Shasta. When they all reached the top, he showed them the hole where he had seen the yellow jackets disappear. Coyote and the Shastas gathered a pile of wood and started a fire and fanned the smoke into the hole, hoping to smoke out the yellow jackets, but the smoke seeped out through vents in the side of the mountain. They scurried around to plug the vents with stones and earth, while Grandfather Turtle crawled to the hole and laid his enormous body over it.

"That should do the trick," said Coyote. "They'll all be dead soon."

They sat down to wait. They heard a distant rumble from deep inside Mount Shasta. The sound came closer, and Grandfather Turtle decided it was time to move. He had just shifted his bulk off the hole when a tremendous explosion blew the top off the mountain and rained fire and smoke and burning rocks and perfectly cooked and smoked salmon all around.

Coyote and Grandfather Turtle and the Shastas gathered the flying salmon and sat down for a feast, courtesy of Mount Shasta's first eruption.

Caucasian Trickster Demi-gods: The Narts

Sosruko Fetches Fire
Kabardian Version, Third Century BC, Adygea

"Nart" means "hero/strong man" and is thought to be cognate with Irish *neart*, meaning "strength". The Narts are demi-god heroes in the mythology of the peoples of the North Caucasus on the northeast coast of the Black Sea. Their superhuman powers and the magical abilities of their horses are similar to those of characters in Irish hero tales and later medieval Indo-European legends of mounted warriors, which scholars say are derived from, or at least strongly influenced by, the Caucasian mythological sagas. Modern Caucasians are still among the most spectacularly athletic horsemen.

According to the stories, the Narts were the first horse riders. Historians, archaeologists, linguists and geneticists agree. There is evidence that horse riding began in the North Caucasus during the Maikop Period, 3700-3000 BC. Groups of riders, apparently Scythians and Cimmerians, passed from the east through the North Caucasus between 850 and 750 BC. Horses had been used as draught animals in Europe since the Bronze Age or earlier, but suddenly about the seventh century BC horse riders appeared in Central Europe. They became known as the Celts. Raiding and trading their way across Europe, they quickly spread in all directions, including back to the east, and by the sixth century BC had become the dominant power in Europe north of the Alps, as well as in Ireland and Britain and most of Spain.

Celtic DNA is widespread among Europeans and people of European descent, especially British and Irish. "Some [pre-Celtic] 'Iberian' blood, possibly, runs through the veins of every modern Englishman, more in the Scots, and in a higher degree in the Welsh and Irish." (Sainero, *Huella*; Trevelyan) Memories of those pre-Celtic horse riders are embodied in the Narts, who are culture heroes of not only the North Caucasians but all of us with European heritage. Curiously, a horse in one Nart story is named "Gee-gee", which is a term of disputed origin used by British and Irish bettors for a race horse.

"Sosruko Fetches Fire" is one of the most popular tales, found in many variants in the languages of the North Caucasus, and is believed to be among the most ancient. It was found on the third century BC Maikop slab but is probably a thousand years older.

The Lady Setenay – matriarch, beautiful temptress, ever-young wise woman – is the mother of all the Narts. Her name means "mother of a hundred sons". She was born of a flower (*Filipendula vulgaris*, dropwort), and the youngest and smallest of her hundred sons had an equally marvellous birth.

As she was washing her clothes in the River Kuban one day, she squatted on the bank in an "unladylike" posture. Sos the cowherd was tending his cattle on the opposite side of the river, and he could not help but notice her exposed private parts. The sight so excited him that he spontaneously ejaculated across the river. His semen landed on a stone next to Setenay. She wrapped the stone in a cloth and took it home and laid it beside the fire.

The stone quickly grew larger, and when she heard noise from inside she took it to the blacksmith Lhepsch. He opened it and found that the sperm of Sos had developed into a flaming baby boy, Sosruko (Son of Sos). Lhepsch held him by the knees with his tongs and dipped him into water seven times to quench the flames and temper his body.

As a result, he was as hard as iron, except for where the tongs had gripped him at the knees; they remained human-like, soft and vulnerable. In contrast to the rest of the Narts, Sosruko was short and dark. Also, iron-like and born of a stone with a cowherd as a father, he was alternately rejected by the others as a freak and an outsider and reluctantly accepted as an invaluable brave and clever problem solver. How he stole fire is an example.

Sosruko was not the original bringer of fire to humans. That was the Nart Nisren-Beard, who took fire from the god Sela at Mount Bashlam (Molten Mount). This is the now-dormant but potentially active 5050m (16,568ft) volcano Mount Kazbek on the border of Georgia and Russia about 100 km north of Tbilisi, which last erupted about 750 BC. In the following story, Sosruko seizes fire from a giant atop Mount Harama, location unspecified, because the Narts had neglected to bring flint and steel with them on a raiding expedition.

The coat of arms of modern Adygea, Sosruko's home territory, depicts him on horseback carrying a firebrand (see Frontispiece). In the background is a twin-peaked mountain resembling the inactive volcano Mount Elbrus, the mountain in the Greek myth where Prometheus stole fire from the gods and was chained by Zeus in punishment. It is the highest mountain in Russia and Europe, lying ten km from the Russian border with Georgia in the ancient Adygea region. One of the rivers that arise in the glaciers of Elbrus is the Kuban, beside which Sosruko was "conceived". It flows north and west from Elbrus through Adygea to the Sea of Azov.

The name of Sosruko's horse, Thozhey, means "little dun" or "little grey". The Nart horses were clever and wise and could speak human, and they feature prominently in many of the tales as advisors and helpers to the heroes.

The giant is a man-eating *emegen*, one of the longstanding enemies of the Narts. Tkha is the supreme god in the pantheon of the Narts. The Abra Stone is a meteorite.

My ballad version of this story is based mainly on an English translation by Amjad Jaimoukha from a Kabardian language text. YouTube has performances of Nart tales, including this one, in a loose ballad form of rhythmic prose, as well as animated versions adapted for children. "Sosruko" has many variant spellings.

The Narts set off to make a raid, Sosruko left behind.
Then suddenly a blizzard struck. "Does anyone have fire?"

They asked. But no one had, and so they suffered, cold and
   shamed
For seven days and seven nights until Sosruko came.

"Sosruko, famed and favourite brother, have you fire?" they
   groaned.
"Of course," said he, and quickly built a blaze to warm their
   bones.
But then the warriors rushed the flame, which irked Sosruko
   so,
He gathered up the embers, and threw them in the snow.

"Golden hero, best of Narts, we'll freeze, as you know well."
"My fellow warriors, never fear. I'll borrow heat from hell."
He mounted Thozhey, battle-hardened, wise and fleet of foot.
"We seek the fire, my stalwart steed, that Nisren-Beard once
   took."

They galloped off until they reached Mount Harama's high
   peak.
He left the horse and crept to see what mischief he could
   wreak.
"A giant is asleep and curled around a massive hearth,"
He told the horse when he returned, and Thozhey said, "Take
   heart.

"Leap on my back, and I will make my hooves like canine
   paws,
And when we near the giant, change to cat pads without
   claws.
You can snatch a burning brand, and we will then escape
And be afar and out of danger when the giant wakes."

Silent as the fog they sneaked into the giant's lair.
Sosruko grabbed a fiery stick – the monster unaware.
The lightning legs of Thozhey flashed down Harama's steep
   side.
The distance from the mountain grew with every flying stride.

For seven days and seven nights without a break they ran,
Until Sosruko lost his grip and dropped the burning brand.
A passing breeze picked up a spark and carried it on high.
It flew to Harama and landed on the giant's thigh.

The giant woke and saw a brand was missing from his hearth.
He roared, "I'll kill the evil thief and eat his living heart."
He stretched an arm out serpent-like along the Seven Roads.
Sosruko, in his week-long flight, could not escape the probe.

The ogre clutched the brave Sosruko, brought him face to
     face
And said, "Young warrior, I admit, you ran a gallant race.
So I won't eat you if you tell me what I want to know:
Inform me where Sosruko is, and then I'll let you go."

"I've heard reports of his great deeds," the wily Nart replies.
"But his location at this time, I fear I can't advise."
"Then give me four examples of the exploits that he's done,
And you won't come to grief if you amuse me with some
     fun."

"Here's one," Sosruko said. "The heavy Abra Stone that
     dropped
From heaven long ago, is tumbled from Kabesky's top.
Sosruko stands below. He catches it upon his brow
And shoots it soaring up again. Let's see you do that now."

"Lead on," the giant said. Sosruko led him to the base
Of Mount Kabesky, then he scrambled up the rocky face.
He sent the weighty fallen star careering down the gorge.
The giant headed it so hard, Sosruko had to dodge.

"My forehead itched," the giant said, "but now the itch is
     scratched.
I liked that one, but can we play a different game of catch?"
Sosruko knew that only Tkha was powerful enough
To kill the beast, but still he carried on his cunning bluff.

40

"Here's another," said the Nart. "Sosruko likes to eat
The heads of arrows shot into his mouth and red with heat."
"I'm getting hungry," said the giant. "This will surely suit."
He opened wide his mammoth maw. "I'm ready," said the
    brute.

Sosruko's inner fire ignited heads of iron red-hot.
He loosed a load of arrows landing in the target spot.
The giant spat the wooden shafts in splinters on the ground,
And then he chewed the arrowheads and swallowed them all
    down.

"That satisfied my hunger pangs, but now I've got the wind."
"I understand," Sosruko said. "When storms arise within,
Sosruko's cure is gulping heated ploughshares made of steel.
Then he poops them out his bum – how good that makes him
    feel."

"Find me some and fire them, Nart, then hide behind a hill."
The giant swallowed white-hot ploughshares till he had his
    fill.
Sosruko, crouching out of sight, could hear the rumbles start.
There rained down shards and shrapnel following a
    thunderous fart.

"Now that my digestion's fixed, show me what is next.
But make it difficult this time, or you could find me vexed."
Only Tkha could bring the contest to a happy end,
And so Sosruko desperately continued to pretend.

"Here is one to challenge you and really test your might.
We need to cross the Seven Gulfs to reach the one that's
    right.
Sosruko stands upon the sea floor, mouth above the waves.
The water of the Gulf is frozen seven nights and days."

"And then?" "To prove how strong he is he squirms his body
    free.
And that is why Sosruko's known as King of the Black Sea."

41

"That's perfect," said the giant, "and I'll carry you across
The Seven Gulfs the sooner I can show you Narts who's
    boss."

Arriving at the seventh Gulf, the giant plunged right in.
His feet were on the bottom, with the water to his chin.
The Nart reversed his inner fire and caused the sea to freeze:
Congealed the water round the giant with his expertise.

For seven days and seven nights the giant seemed entrapped.
Sosruko said, "Now try to move." The ice began to crack.
"Too soon, my friend," Sosruko said. "You need a little
    longer.
One more hour in the ice will make you that much stronger."

The giant stayed. Sosruko prayed to the almighty god:
"O, Tkha, please help me keep the Gulf ice solid and
    unthawed."
He worked again to freeze the Gulf. This time it set like rock.
"Now, giant, move." The giant tried. "I can't!" he said in
    shock.

Sosruko drew his sword, the helpless monster's head to hew.
"I was a fool," the giant said. "Sosruko, it is you.
I should have noticed Lhepsch's tong-marks when I saw your
    knees."
The giant sent him flying far with one propulsive wheeze.

It took Sosruko half a day to run back, it is said.
He swung his sword to make the giant shorter by a head.
He brought the fire-brand to the Narts, who huddled in a
    heap.
Some had died from cold and others smothered by the heat.

The fire revived them. They continued on their plundering
    way.
They praised Sosruko: "Fearless leader, you have saved the
    day."

(There are more stories about those thinking/talking Nart horses in my book *Hellhounds and Hero Horses: Beasts of Myth and Legend.*)

Shirdon and the Giants
Ossetia, Caucasus

Nart Shirdon was walking through the forest one day when he came upon three giants fighting. He asked them what the problem was.

"We have these three things here," one of them said, "and we can't agree how to share them.

"There's this skin. All you have to do is sit on it and make a wish, and it will take you wherever you want to go. There's this three-legged table. If you hit it with a felt whip, it will be covered with all kinds of food and drink. There's this rope. Tie up any treasures you have and they will be lighter."

"I have a solution," said Shirdon. "Each of you give me an arrow, and I'll shoot them in different directions. Whoever comes back first with the arrow gets first choice of these things. The second gets second choice, and the third gets what's left."

They agreed. Shirdon shot the arrows far far in different directions, and the giants ran after them. While they were gone, Shirdon put the table on the skin and tied it with the rope, sat on the skin, and wished he was on the roof of his house many miles away.

When he landed, he struck the table with a felt whip, and there appeared a feast that he shared with his friends and neighbours.

Irish Trickster Demi-gods

Gobán Saor and the Monks

"Gobán" is related to "smith", but it comes from the name of one of the Irish god-figures, Goibhniu, who was a master builder. "Gobán Saor" can be best translated as "freelance builder", but many stories about him use "Gobán" as his first name, like Goibhniu.

There are two round towers at the sixth-century monastery of Clonmacnoise. One is finished, and the other lacks a cap. This is why.

The monks asked Gobán to build a second tower to match the one already there. Just as he was putting the finishing touches on the top, the monks asked how much he was going to charge. He told them, and they said it was too much. He said he wouldn't take any less. They took away the ladder and said, "When you come down in your price, you can come down from the tower."

Gobán started to deconstruct the tower, throwing the blocks down to the ground, and the monks relented, but Gobán refused to finish the job. Perhaps it was that experience that led him to develop a technique for working on the upper stories of timber buildings without a ladder: he would throw a nail into the air and a hammer after it in such a way that the hammer would drive the nail into the required location.

Gobán Saor and the King of Spain

He was hired once by the King of Spain to build the most magnificent palace in the world. Gobán and his son set off for Spain, but along the way, he got bored and asked his son to shorten the road. The lad had no idea what that meant and remained silent. Gobán said, "Well, then, we'll go back home." That happened the next day as well, and Gobán's wife asked her son why they kept returning.

44

"Father wants me to shorten the road, and I don't know how to do that."

"It's simple. He means you should tell stories so that the journey doesn't seem so long."

(The motto of Storytellers of Ireland is "Two Shorten the Road / *Giorraíonn beirt bóthar*," and the logo shows two people walking while one is telling a story.)

So the following day, when Gobán said, "Shorten the road," the boy told stories, and they continued on to Spain.

They had nearly finished building the palace, when an Irish servant of the king warned Gobán that the king planned to kill them both so that they would not be able to build a palace for another king to rival his. Gobán called the king and told him to look directly up along the wall of the castle.

"See how the top of the wall leans out? It's a bit crooked, and I'll need to straighten it so it doesn't fall down. I have a tool at home for just that job, and we'll have to go and get it."

(It was an optical illusion. If you look straight up the wall of any building, it looks as if it is going to fall.)

The king refused to let them go, suspecting that they knew he planned to kill them.

"I'll send my son instead," the king said. "Tell him the name of the tool, and he'll bring it back."

"It's called *cor in aghaidh an caim*," Gobán said. "It means 'a twist against the crooked'."

(It does, literally, but *cor* also means "to slip", as in to give someone the slip; *cam* also means "fraud" – crookedness in a person.)

When the king's son gave Gobán's wife the message, she correctly deduced that her husband and her son were in danger, and she construed the name of the non-existent tool as an order to detain the king's son.

"It's a big, heavy tool," she said. "I can't lift it, so you'll have to take it out of that chest yourself."

When the king's son bent over and reached in to the chest, she picked up his legs and tipped him into it, closing the lid and locking it. She sent a message to the king to say

45

that she would release his son when her husband and son arrived home safely.

Craftsmen used to carve their personal logo into their works when they finished. Gobán's symbol was a two-tailed cat, which you can still see on many medieval castles and churches in Ireland. Telling a story to shorten the road also appears in a Nart tale.

The Narrow-striped Kern

Manannán mac Lir in Ireland and Scotland – Manawydan fab Llŷr in Wales, Mannin in the Isle of Man – is the ubiquitous Celtic sea god personage in these islands, euhemerized as a famous sea trader. He is associated with the Irish god-like Tuatha Dé Danann (Tribes of the Goddess Dana), but is not one of them, and is a sometime rival of the chief Danann, the Dagda Mór. He is a magician and shape-shifter, a trickster and teacher/tester, a protector and enabler. His main alter egos are the Narrow-striped Kern (itinerant mercenary foot-soldier) and the Giolla Deacair (the Difficult Servant).

The historical Black Hugh O'Donnell was lord of Tirconnell, modern County Donegal, from 1505 until his death in 1537. My version of this story is based on a 19th-century Irish manuscript and Standish Hayes O'Grady's translation in *Silva Gadelica*. O'Grady says it was composed during O'Donnell's lifetime or shortly thereafter, and that named characters were real people, contemporaries of O'Donnell, though the actions attributed to them are fictional. O'Donnell has been co-opted as a character in other folk tales.

Douglas Hyde (1860-1949) was a folk tale and song collector before he became the first president of Ireland. In his book *Beside the Fire* (1890), he says that this tale was a widely known stock piece in the repertoires of Irish and Scottish storytellers "told to this day without any great variations".

46

Dún Mona, now called Dunstaffnage Castle, is in Argyll and Bute near Oban in western Scotland. Sídh Fionnachaidh is a cairn, an entrance to the Otherworld, on Deadman's Hill (Slieve Fuad) in County Armagh near Newtownhamilton. Aileach of the Kings is Grianán Aileach, a hillfort in Inishowen in County Donegal.

Black Hugh O'Donnell and his nobles were having a feast in Ballyshannon one day, when a Kern entered the banquet hall wearing narrow stripes, with puddle-water splashing in his boots, the tops of both ears sticking out of a ragged cloak, a naked sword protruding behind him, and three charred javelins made of holly in his right hand.

"God bless you, O'Donnell," he said.

"God bless yourself," replied O'Donnell. "Where do you come from, uncouth fellow?"

"In Dún Mona in the town of the king of Scotland I slept last night," said the Kern. "I do be a day in Islay, a day in Kintyre, a day in the Isle of Man, a day in Rathlin, and another day in the watch-seat at Sídh Fionnachaidh on Slieve Fuad. I am a pleasant, peripatetic, precocious person, and now I am your guest, O'Donnell."

"Bring me the gatekeeper," ordered O'Donnell.

When the gatekeeper arrived, O'Donnell said, "Did you let this man in?"

"It wasn't me. I've never seen him before."

"Leave him alone, O'Donnell," said the Kern, "for I come and go as I please."

"Sit down," said O'Donnell.

"I sit or not sit as the fancy takes me."

Then the Kern turned to the court harpers and said, "Play us a tune, Conán Maolrua O'Raferty," and Conán played a fine piece.

"Play us a tune, Diarmaid O'Gilligán."

Diarmaid played.

"Play us a tune, Cormac O'Cieragán and Taig O'Crugadán."

They all played well, and the fine fairylike flow of sound was pleasing to the company. But the Kern said,

"Never since I heard the sledge-hammers of Hell slamming the iron have I listened to such cacophony as your people make, O'Donnell."

He picked up a harp and started to play. The sounds that streamed from the strings would send sleep to a woman in labour and heal the wounds of warriors and soothe the sicknesses of the whole world.

"I have never heard sweeter music," said O'Donnell. "You are surely a melodious rogue."

"Some days I'm sweet, some days I'm sour," said the Kern.

The butler came to the Kern and said, "O'Donnell has invited you to his table. Come up and join him."

"I won't," said the Kern. "I'd rather be the ugly rascal playing tricks on the noble gentlemen. But if it pleases them, they could send down something of benefit to me."

The butler brought him a waistcoat, a cap, a striped shirt and a cloak, saying, "Here is a suit that O'Donnell sent you."

"I won't accept it," said the Kern. "I don't want any noble person to have a claim on me."

Twenty armed horsemen were placed outside on both sides of the entrance, and twenty Scottish mercenaries inside the doors, for they realized that the Kern was not a man of this world.

"What is all this for?" the Kern asked.

"To keep you here with us," said O'Donnell.

"By the three sureties of God," said the Kern, "what use is it to try to keep me here, when I won't be taking my lunch with you tomorrow?"

"Where, then?" said O'Donnell.

"At Cnoc Áine [Knockainy], twelve miles outside of Limerick, where Seán mac an Iarla is."

"I swear to God," said one of the Scottish soldiers, "if I catch you moving before morning I'll beat you into a lump with the butt of my battle-axe."

The Kern put his hand to a harp and began to pluck out sweet tunes and soft melodies that would put the world to sleep. Then he called out, "Soldiers, where are you? I'm coming out now, so watch carefully or I'll get away from you."

When the soldiers heard this, they thought they saw him coming and began to flail their battle-axes so that they only knocked each other to the ground. Then the mounted men joined in, until they all lay unmoving in pools of blood.

The Kern came out without a mark on him. He told the gatekeeper to tell O'Donnell that he would bring the men back to life in exchange for twenty cows and a cartron (thirty acres) of land. He gave the gatekeeper some herbs and told him to rub them on the men's gums, which he did, and the men stood up whole and healthy. So the Kern got his cows and cartron of land from O'Donnell.

At that moment, Seán mac an Iarla (Mac Gearailt, ie, Fitzgerald) of Desmond happened to be holding an assembly on the green in front of his fort. He looked up and saw the Narrow-striped Kern coming toward him, with his naked blade sticking out the back and water streaming from his old shoes and the tops of his two ears poking through his ragged cape and a javelin made of a bulrush in his hand.

"God bless you," said the Kern.

"God bless yourself," said Seán. "Have you come far, fellow?"

"Last night I slept in the house of O'Donnell, the night before in Dún Mona in the town of the king of Scotland, and tonight you have me as your guest, Son of the Earl."

"What is your name?"

"Durtane O'Durtane is my forename and surname."

"What way did you come here?"

"By Ess Rua in Sligo, by the lovely lush Cess Coráinn, from there to the Curlew Hills and thence to Magh Lurg of the Dagda, round the hill of Rathcroghan [those four in County Roscommon], to Magh Mucrimne [in County Galway], to the territory of O'Conaill Gabra [western County Limerick], and now to your hospitality, Seán mac an Iarla."

49

Seán took him inside, where he had a drop of a drink, washed his feet, and went to bed and slept till sunrise the next day. Seán came to him in the morning and said affectionately, "You've slept long, though it's no wonder with the long walk you had. I've heard that you are clever at reading and at harping, and I'd like to hear a sample of that this morning."

"I'm very accomplished at those arts," said the Kern. He picked up a book, but he couldn't read a word. He picked up a harp, but he couldn't play a tune.

"It seems that your talents for reading and music have deserted you," said Seán.

Stung by the criticism, the Kern grabbed an old lore-book of Seán's and read it with scholarly skill and euphonious enunciation. Then he picked up a harp and played a sweet and delicate flowing mellifluous melody that could banish all sickness and ill-health from the world. The mellow soft-warm fairy tune could send rest and repose to all.

"It is truly the talented man you are, Durtane," said Seán.

"Some days I'm sweet, some days I'm sour," said Durtane.

At midday, Seán took Durtane out on to Cnoc Áine.

"Have you ever been on this hill before, Durtane?"

"I have. And I remember the time I joined with Fionn mac Cumhaill and his son Oisín and Oisín's son Oscar and the rest of the Fianna, hunting the hare and the fox and the fowl and chasing the badger and the deer, until Fionn's hounds, dulcet-toned Bran and sweet-singing Sceolán, pursued a red and white deer in the direction of Slieve Luachra and were lost to sight."

Seán was looking in the direction of Slieve Luachra, and when he turned to speak to the Kern he had disappeared, and Seán never knew to which quarter of the world he had vanished.

The chief poet of Leinster, Mac Eochaid (McKeogh), had been lying in bed for eighteen weeks with a broken leg that oozed blood and marrow, which the twelve best doctors in Leinster were unable to cure. Suddenly, he saw a soldier in narrow stripes wearing a tatty cloak with a book in his hand and humming a song.

"God bless you, Mac Eochaid," said the Kern.

"God bless yourself," said Mac Eochaid. "Have you come far, fellow?"

"I slept last night in the house of Seán mac an Iarla of Desmond. In the house of O'Donnell in Ballyshannon I slept the previous night. I was born in Aileach of the Kings. I do be a day in Islay, a day in Kintyre, a day in the Isle of Man, a day in Rathlin, and another day in the watch-seat at Sídh Fionnachaidh on Slieve Fuad. For I am a pleasant, precocious, perennially peripatetic perambulator."

"What is your name?"

"Cathal O'Cain is my forename and surname."

"What skills do you have?"

"I am a journeyman healer, and if you lay aside the inhospitality, stinginess and all-round cantankerdsomeness that's in you, I can heal your leg."

"Those are in me, to be sure, until I've had three drinks," said Mac Eochaid. "After that, I don't care what anyone does."

"Will you follow my advice?"

"I will."

Cathal took out a healing herb and applied it to Mac Eochaid's leg and said, "Rise up, Mac Eochaid, till we see if you have a run in you."

Mac Eochaid stood up and set off across the plain with the rest of his people chasing, and soon out-paced the twelve doctors behind him.

"I've cured you, Mac Eochaid," said Cathal. "But if you return to your vices and bad manners I'll come back and break that leg again, and the other one as well, and all the doctors in the world now and in the past and in future will not be able to mend them."

"I won't," said Mac Eochaid. "I have a beautiful daughter I'll give you, along with three hundred cows,

51

three hundred horses, three hundred sheep, and three hundred pigs. You'll be my son-in-law."

"Fine," said Cathal. "Be she fair or foul, I'll have her."

Mac Eochaid laid on a big feast in honour of the occasion, but in the commotion and confusion, the Kern absconded across the hills. When Mac Eochaid learned this, he said, "The next person who hosts Cathal O'Cain will be a lucky man."

The Kern never stopped nor stayed until he reached Sligo just as O'Connor was setting off with his army to avenge the theft of the hag of Connacht's basket by the hag of Munster. O'Connor saw the Narrow-striped Kern coming toward him.

"God bless you," said the Kern.

"God bless yourself," said O'Connor. "Have you come far?"

"Yesterday I was in Leinster in the house of Mac Eochaid. I spent the night before that twelve miles from Limerick at Cnoc Áine in the house of Seán mac an Iarla. In the house of O'Donnell in Ballyshannon I slept the previous night, and the night before that in Dún Mona in the town of the king of Scotland. I was born in Aileach of the Kings. I do be a day in Islay, a day in Kintyre, a day in the Isle of Man, a day in Rathlin, and another day in the watch-seat at Sídh Fionnachaidh on Slieve Fuad. For I am a pleasant, precocious, perennially peripatetic perambulator."

"What's your name?" said O'Connor.

"The Giolla Deacair. Might I ask where you are all going?"

"We're going to do battle with Munster."

"If you hire me, I'll go with you."

One of O'Connor's kerns said, "Not only will we not hire you, you couldn't pay us to let you come with us."

"It's not you I'm asking, it's O'Connor. And it will perhaps not be the worst for him for me to be with him."

"What payment do you want, Giolla Deacair?" said O'Connor.

"I ask no more but that nothing unfair be done to me while I'm with you."

"Agreed," said O'Connor.

The Connachtmen went in to Munster and harried the kingdom until they gathered and made off with herds of horses and cows and flocks of sheep, along with the Munster hag's three dappled cows and her hornless bull, which O'Connor gave to the Connacht hag as compensation for the loss of her basket.

They were not long driving their prey before they saw the Munster warriors pursuing them and the animals. The Giolla Deacair went to O'Connor and said, "Which do you want me to do: drive the herds or hold off the pursuers?"

"Hold off the pursuers," said O'Connor.

The Giolla Deacair took a bow and 24 arrows, and there was not one arrow that didn't fell nine times nine of the Munstermen, until none of them dared to venture within range. While he was doing that, the Connachtmen had managed to drive just twenty of the cattle not even as far as the flight of an arrow. O'Connor asked the Giolla Deacair to help drive the herds.

He swiftly rounded up the animals and sped them on toward Connacht, but when the Munstermen saw that his back was to them, they began to slaughter the Connachtmen, and the Giolla Deacair returned to rearguard action. So between the herding and the harrying, they got the animals across the Shannon and into Sligo to O'Connor's fort.

O'Connor was the first inside. They put a drink in his hand, and he drank it down without consideration for the Giolla Deacair. The Giolla Deacair announced that he was leaving. This made O'Connor realize that he had offended his guest by not offering him a drink first, thereby violating his agreement that nothing unjust would be done to him, and he told him that he would give him a special reward. The Giolla Deacair declined the offer and spoke this verse before he disappeared:

Slighting me, O mighty chief,
reveals in thee discourtesy.
To snub the Kern whose efforts earned
the Munster raid – 'twas ill repaid.

At this time it happened that Tadg O'Kelly was holding an assembly at his fort in his fine town in Hy-Many (parts of Counties Galway and Roscommon). He saw the Narrow-striped Kern approaching, with his naked sword protruding behind him and the tips of his two ears poking through a worn cloak and his old shoes sloshing with water.

"God bless you," said the Kern.

"God bless yourself," said O'Kelly. "Have you come far?"

"In the house of O'Connor in Sligo I slept last night, and in Mac Eochaid's house in Leinster the night before, and in the house of Seán mac an Iarla the previous night, in the house of O'Donnell in Ballyshannon the night before that, and in the town of the king of Scotland before that. I was born in Aileach of the Kings. I do be a day in Islay, a day in Kintyre, a day in the Isle of Man, and a day in Rathlin, and a day in the watch-seat at Sídh Fionnachaidh on Slieve Fuad. For I am a pleasant, precocious, perennially peripatetic perambulator."

"What talents do you have?" said O'Kelly.

"I am a prestidigitator, and if you give me five marks, I'll show you a trick."

"I'll give you that," said O'Kelly.

The Kern placed three straws on the palm of his hand.

"I will blow the middle straw off my hand without moving the other two."

"Let's see you do that," said O'Kelly.

The Kern set the tips of two fingers on the two outer straws and blew the middle one off.

"And there you have the trick," said the Kern.

"By my conscience, that wasn't a bad trick," said O'Kelly.

"No credit to the man who did that," said one of O'Kelly's soldiers. "Give me half of the five marks, and I'll do the trick."

"Do that trick the same way," said the Kern, "and I'll give you half of the five marks."

The soldier placed three straws on the palm of his hand, and he put the tips of two fingers on the two outer straws, but when he blew on the middle straw the tips of his fingers went through the palm of his hand and came out the back of it.

"No, no, man," said the narrow-striped conjuror. "That was clumsy, and it's not the way I did it. But since you lost the money, I'll mend the damage."

The conjuror rubbed a healing herb on the man's hand until it was fully restored.

"Now, Tadg O'Kelly," said the conjuror. "Give me another five marks and I'll show you another trick."

"What trick is that?"

"I can wag one of my ears without moving the other one."

"Show us."

The trickster took one of his ears in his hand and wagged it.

"That was indeed a good trick," said O'Kelly.

"No credit to you," said the same soldier. "With any luck I'll do that trick."

"You failed with the other one," said the Narrow-striped Kern. "Let's see you try this one."

The soldier succeeded in wagging his ear, but it came off in his hand.

"That was clumsy of your soldier, O'Kelly," said the conjuror, "but I'll mend him, and for another five marks I'll show you another trick."

"Go ahead," said O'Kelly.

The conjuror took a ball of silk yarn out of his bag of tricks and, holding the end of the thread, threw the ball up into the air until it stuck in a cloud. Then he took a hare out of the bag and sent it running up the thread, then he took a small red-eared hound out of the bag and sent it chasing after the hare, then he took a young man out of the bag and told him to run up the thread after the hound and the hare, and then he took a beautiful and shapely young woman out of another bag and told her to follow the man and the hound and to make sure the hound didn't abuse the hare. She quickly ran up the thread, and it was a pleasure for Tadg O'Kelly to gaze after them all and listen to the sounds of the chase coming from the cloud. Soon there was silence.

"I'm afraid there is some mischief being done up there," said the conjuror.

"Of what sort?" said O'Kelly.

"I think the hound has eaten the hare and the man is with the woman."

"That's only natural," said O'Kelly.

The conjuror pulled the thread, and they all came tumbling down: the hound gnawing the bones of the hare and the man embracing the woman. The conjuror was furious, and he took out his sword and brought it down on the man's neck and cut off his head. O'Kelly objected to such a deed done in his presence.

"If that bothers you, I'll fix it," said the conjuror.

He picked up the head and threw it at the man's body. It stuck, and the man stood up, but his head was on backwards.

"He would be better off dead than living like that," said O'Kelly.

The conjuror grabbed the man and twisted his head so that it was the right way round, and he was as whole and healthy as he had been before. Tadg O'Kelly turned away for a moment, and when he looked again the conjuror had disappeared, to what part of the world he never knew.

A feast of celebration was happening at that time in the house of the king of Leinster. They saw the Narrow-striped Kern coming toward them, the water sloshing about in his old shoes and his naked sword sticking out behind him.

"God bless you," said the Kern.

"God bless yourself," said the king of Leinster. "Have you come far?"

"I've just come from the house of Tadg O'Kelly. In the house of O'Connor in Sligo I spent the previous night. I was born at Aileach of the Kings. I do be a day in Islay and a day in Kintyre, a day in the Isle of Man and a day in Rathlin and a day in the watch-seat at Sídh Fionnachaidh on Slieve Fuad. I am a pleasant, peripatetic, precocious person."

"What is your name?" said the king of Leinster.

"The Giolla Deacair."

Sixteen men were playing harps.

"By my word," said the Giolla Deacair, "never since the noise of the hammers in the hollows of Hell have I heard such a massacre of music."

"You filthy scoundrel," said the brawniest of the harpers. "You have no right to say that to us."

"I assure you," said the Giolla Deacair, "as bad as the other fifteen are, you are far worse."

The harper took his sword and brought it down on the Giolla Deacair's head and split him in two – or so he thought. What really happened was that it was his own head that the stroke fell on, and the two halves of him fell to one side and the other. Then the other fifteen harpers tried to kill the Giolla Deacair, but they met with the same fate.

The king of Leinster ordered his household guard to take the evildoer out and hang him, and they did so, but when they returned to the king they saw the Giolla Deacair.

"Didn't we just hang you?" they said.

"Go and look," he replied.

They went back to the gibbet and found the body of the king's favourite guard dangling on the rope. Three more times they tried to hang the Giolla Deacair, killing three more of the king's favourites in his place.

He spent the night in the king of Leinster's house – only because they didn't dare throw him out – and in the morning he went to the king and said, "I killed some of your men yesterday, but I'll bring them back to life now."

"I'm glad of that," said the king.

He made them whole and healthy again, and then he took a harp and played such sweet fairy tunes that would relieve the whole world of sickness and sorrow. The king glanced at his own musicians, and when he turned back to the Giolla Deacair, he had disappeared.

He neither loitered nor lingered until he reached Seán O'Donnellan's house in Kilskeer in Meath. There they fed him a cup of curdled milk and a plate of crab-apples, and when he finished he went away, and no one knew in which direction. That was the last anyone heard of the Narrow-striped Kern.

Lady Gregory tells this story in her book *Gods and Fighting Men* (1904), and there are traces of it in her play *Dervorgilla* (1907), about the woman over whom two Irish kings quarrelled, leading to the 12th-century Anglo-Norman invasion:

> Dervorgilla: Where do you come from, boy?
> Songmaker: From the province of Connacht I am come. Connacht yesterday, Armagh tomorrow. To-day it is Mellifont has got hold of me. ... one day sweet, another day sour.
> Dervorgilla: Will the generations to come think better of me, thinking me to have been taken as a prey, like the Connacht hag's basket, or the Munster hag's speckled cow?

Douglas Hyde said that O'Connor of Sligo invaded Munster in 1362. I am not aware of a tale about the theft of the hag of Connacht's basket by the hag of Munster. I have searched my library, the National Folklore Collection and the internet, and consulted several Irish folklorists without success. There are two possibilities: the tale was so popular in the 16th century that the author of this story

58

thought it unnecessary to tell it, and it has now been lost; or the author was spoofing and the tale never existed. If that is so, it seems that the author couldn't resist playing a trick of his own and sending the reader/listener on a wild goose chase.

Tricking the Devil

This is a small sample of the many international tales in which the Ultimate Trickster, a Christianized version of an evil demi-god, is defeated by human cleverness.

How the Devil Made the Lousberg
Aachen, Germany

A young German tourist told this story about 1995 at a storytelling session in Dublin.

A proud architect was building a cathedral in Aachen, and he wanted it to have the highest steeple in the world. The challenge was beyond his ability, so he made a pact with the Devil in exchange for the soul of the first living thing to enter the cathedral when it was finished. He made sure that a dog entered before any human. The Devil was angry at being tricked, and he came to Aachen bent on revenge, but the people recognized him by his cloven hooves and chased him away.

Now doubly incensed, he went to the Sahara and gathered a huge amount of sand in a special magic sack with the intention of burying the city. He trudged and trudged, and finally even his great preternatural strength began to give out. He set the sack down to rest, unaware that he was less than a kilometre from Aachen (which was much smaller then).

A woman whose job it was to collect shoes for repair and then return them to the owners came along carrying a bag of worn shoes. The Devil asked her how far it was to Aachen. She noticed his cloven hooves and suspected trouble.

"Ach," she said, opening her bag, "I'm on my way home from Aachen, and I've walked so far I've worn out all these shoes."

Discouraged, the Devil returned to Hell, leaving the 264-metre high sack of sand. It's now covered with trees and called the Lousberg, on the north side of Aachen, from which you can enjoy a fine view of the now-sprawling city thanks to the Devil. There is also a sculpture of himself and the shoe woman on the hill, which proves that this story is true.

A similar thing happened in Britain, and that's how the Isle of Wight was formed.

G303.9.2. The devil performs deeds of unusual strength.

K219.6. Devil gets an animal in place of a human being.

H241. Worn-out shoes as proof of long journey.

The Devil's Wager
Asturias, Spain

Saint Crispin was a leather worker living in Gaul who preached the Gospel in the third century and was beheaded during the reign of Diocletian. His feast day is 25 October.

One day, he decided to try his hand at farming. He ploughed and cultivated a field and planted cabbages, carrots, peas and turnips, which all grew and flourished magnificently and which he shared with poor people who had no land to grow food. The Devil noticed this and was envious. He ploughed and cultivated a field next to Crispin's, and when it was ready for planting he came to see Crispin.

"Well, Crispin," said the Devil, "you see that I've become a farmer as well. The work is good for the health, and the harvest is like honey on pastry, like icing on the cake."

Crispin suspected by the look in his eye that some trickery was afoot.

"Yes. A good harvest is a good thing," he said noncommittally.

"Exactly. And wouldn't it be even better if your harvest could be combined with mine?"

"What do you mean by that?"

"I propose a wager. I will sow seeds in my field. When they have matured, if you can identify the plants correctly in no more than three attempts, all my harvest will go into your barn. On the other hand, if you can't identify them, all your harvest will go into my barn."

This seemed good to Crispin. With two harvests he would have that much more to share with the poor people, and so he accepted the Devil's wager.

Crispin visited all his farmer neighbours, and when he saw a plant he didn't recognize he asked what it was: French bean, artichoke, aubergine, parsnip, spinach, leek, cucumber, chickpea, and many more. Very soon he knew more about plants than Solomon himself.

However, and not surprisingly, the Devil cheated. He went to Argentina and got some seeds of *zapallito de tronco* – a summer squash like zucchini. When Crispin went to see how the Devil's crop was growing, he had no idea what the plants were.

The Devil saw him and said, "So, Crispin. When are you going to tell me what crop is growing here?"

"Wait till harvest time," said Crispin. He racked his brain to come up with a way of discovering the name of the plant. One morning, just as he was about to give up, an idea struck him. He went to the Devil and said, "You'd better stand guard over your field. Last night I was looking at it trying to work out what the crop was, and I saw a strange beast walking around in the middle of it."

The Devil was pleased that Crispin hadn't identified the crop yet, but he worried that the beast might damage it, and he would lose his wager. So he stood guard the following night.

Meanwhile, Crispin got a bucket of honey and a sack of feathers and poured the honey over himself and then the feathers, so that he looked like nothing ever seen in nature. He went to the Devil's field and hid himself watching for the appearance of the Devil. When the Devil arrived, Crispin jumped out of his hiding place and ran around the field roaring and screaming.

The Devil was nearly frightened out of his skin, but he shouted, "Go away, monster. You're trampling on my zapallitos de tronco."

Crispin ran off.

When the day came that both Crispin's and the Devil's crops were ready to be harvested, the Devil arrived at Crispin's house and said, "Crispin, do you know why I'm here?"

"I do."

"You remember our little wager?"

"I do."

"Well, then, you have three guesses. What is the name of the plants in my field?"

"Cabbage."

"Wrong. Two more guesses."

"Salt wort."

"Wrong again," said the Devil, rubbing his hands with glee. "Your last guess?"

"Zapallito de tronco."

The Devil let out a bellow of rage that could be heard all over the district, and he ran off like a scalded hare.

K216.2.1. Guessing name of devil's secret plant. The man's wife in tar and feathers overhears the devil tell the secret name of the crop he has discovered (tobacco). The devil says to the supposed animal, "Get out of my tobacco!"

The Man with No Shadow
Salamanca, Spain; Navarre, Basque Country

The vaulted c. 16th-century portico and recently renovated entrance to the Cave of Salamanca can be seen beneath the Plaza de Carvajal on Cuesta de Carvajal near Calle San Pablo on the south side of the city behind the cathedral and downhill from it. A secret tunnel is said to connect the Cave with the crypt of the cathedral. It was closed by royal order in the 15th century "to put a stop to superstitious rumours".

63

A variant of the first part of this story is current in Salamanca, with the 15th-century Marqués de Villena as the hero. The Cave is also known as the Cave of San Cipriano for its association with that converted wizard, whose purported book of magic spells is the subject of the chapter "O Ciprianillo". The famous 13th-century Scottish wizard Michael Scot was a visitor:

> When in Salamanca's cave
> Him listed his magic wand to wave
> The bells would ring in Notre Dame.

During the Middle Ages, Satan himself used the Cave to hold night classes in the black arts for those studying for the priesthood at the university. The agreed payment for their tuition was that one member of the class would remain with their master as his servant when the course was finished. Don Juan de Atarrabio from Goñi in Navarre, who was pursuing both curricula, and his classmates made a plan to circumvent this.

After the final night of classes, the students filed out of the Cave into the bright morning sunshine. The Devil stood at the entrance, which faces east, and as each man passed him he said, "Are you going to stay with me?"

As they had arranged among themselves, each student said, "Take the one behind me."

Don Juan was at the end of the line. Satan was counting, and he knew that Juan should be the last, but when he said, "Are you going to stay with me?" and Juan replied, "Take the one behind me," Satan thought he had miscounted. He could see Juan's shadow behind him, and in the unaccustomed glare of the sunlight he mistook it for "the one behind". He brought his sword down sharply behind Juan as he passed, cutting off his shadow. Juan and the others escaped safely.

The Devil was annoyed at being left without a servant, but he was satisfied that Juan would end up in his clutches eventually, for it is well known that a person without a shadow cannot enter Heaven.

When Don Juan finished his studies at the university, he served as priest in Goñi, about twelve miles (20km) west of Pamplona, where he lived with his mother. Of course it was soon noticed that he had no shadow, but he was a good priest and popular with the people, so they quickly got used to this slight deformity, though they regretted that they would not be able to meet him in the afterlife. One reason he was so popular was that he was able to make good use of the knowledge he had gained in the Devil's school. Here are two examples.

The weather had been unusually fine one year. The wheat was standing tall and thick in the fields ready to be harvested, and the local farmers were expecting a bumper crop. One day as Don Juan was about to take a siesta he noticed a huge black cloud in the distance. He said to his mother, "If that cloud comes closer, wake me up before you hear thunder."

But his mother forgot to keep an eye on the cloud, and it was looming over the town before she noticed it and woke her son. Don Juan leapt out of bed, and he heard the voice of the Devil from the cloud:

"I have some little horses that are going to trample your wheat."

The priest held a book of magic spells in one hand and a crucifix in the other and said, "And I have some small reins that will control your horses."

The cloud burst open and poured down rain and hailstones, but through Don Juan's magic power all the rain and hail was directed into a large number of barrels that stood next to the cemetery, and so the wheat crop was saved.

Another time, Don Juan received a divine message in his head: the Pope in Rome was in danger and Don Juan's help was needed immediately. Satan himself in the form of a beautiful woman had so bewitched the Pope that the Pope was going to ask Satan to marry him. Don Juan called up three demons that were at his service and asked the first one, "How soon can you take me to Rome?"

The demon answered, "Fifteen minutes."

"Not good enough. And you?" he asked the second demon.

"Five minutes."

"Not good enough. And you?"

"As soon as we start we will be there," replied the third demon.

"You'll do," said the priest. "Let's go."

"What will you pay me for this?" asked the demon.

"I'll give you the uppermost part of my dinner tonight," Don Juan said, knowing what his mother planned to serve. The demon accepted this, and they had no sooner set off than they arrived at the Vatican. Don Juan knocked at the door. When the porter opened it, Don Juan said, "Take me to the Pope immediately."

"I'm sorry, that's impossible," said the porter. "His Holiness is entertaining a visitor for dinner."

Don Juan handed the porter a staff with a cross carved on it that he had brought for the purpose.

"I want you to take this and measure the length and width of the table where the Holy Father and his guest are eating."

The porter did this, and as soon as he placed the staff across the width of the table after measuring the length – thereby making the Sign of the Cross – the beautiful woman gave a shriek and disappeared in a puff of smoke. The Pope understood immediately what had happened, and he asked the porter who had given him the staff and told him to measure the table.

"It was a priest at the door who wanted to come in to see you."

"Send him in now," said the Pope.

But Don Juan had already left. On the way home, he and the demon flew through a snowstorm, and when he entered the kitchen where his mother was serving his dinner, he shook the snow off his cloak.

"I didn't know it was snowing," his mother said.

"It's snowing in the Jaca mountains," said Don Juan.

"I don't believe that," his mother said.

"It's as true as the fact that that chicken you have roasted can sing," said Don Juan. At that, the roasted chicken sat up and began to crow.

Don Juan took a small plate and scraped off the uppermost portion of the food that was set at his place at the table. His mother had cooked a dish based on nuts, and as was her custom she had put the nutshells on the top of the food as a decoration. This is what Don Juan took outside as the payment he had promised for the demon that had flown him to Rome.

As Don Juan grew older and closer to the time when he would have to account for his life, he began to worry that he would not go to Heaven when he died because he had no shadow. However, he had noticed that when he celebrated Mass, at the moment of the Consecration his shadow appeared briefly and then disappeared again. He explained his problem to the sacristan and told him that his only hope of getting into Heaven was for the sacristan to kill him at the moment of the Consecration, when his shadow appeared.

The sacristan was horrified and refused to have anything to do with the plan. But Don Juan pressed him and wrote out a letter that explained the situation and exonerated the sacristan from any responsibility. The sacristan finally agreed to do what Don Juan wanted.

Don Juan said, "Take a big hammer, and at the moment of the Consecration, when you see my shadow appear, hit me hard on the head. Then cut open my chest and take out my heart and nail it still bleeding to the door of the church. If you see a black bird take my heart, you will know that my soul has gone to Hell, but if a white bird takes it, that will be a sign that I am in Heaven."

The following morning at the Consecration the sacristan did what he had agreed, and when Don Juan was dead the sacristan cut out his heart and nailed it to the door of the church. Immediately a large flock of ravens swooped into the plaza in front of the church and began circling. But suddenly a small white dove shot straight down from Heaven, took the priest's heart in its beak, and soared straight up again until it was out of sight.

S241.2. Devil is to have last one who leaves "black school".

K525.2. Man steps aside so that only his shadow is caught.

G303.3.1.12.2. Devil as a beautiful young woman seduces man.

B171. Magic chicken (hen, cock).

Sæmundr the Learned and the Devil
Iceland

Like Don Juan de Atarrabio, Sæmundr the Learned (1056–1133), the earliest historian of Iceland, attended the Devil's school while he was studying for the priesthood on the Continent, and he also lost his shadow when he made his escape. He went on to trick the Devil in a number of ways.

When Sæmundr and two fellow Icelandic students left the school, they heard that the directorship of the education centre at Oddi in Iceland was open. Whoever reached the centre first would get the position. Sæmundr called the Devil and promised him his soul if he swam with him on his back to Iceland, on condition that Sæmundr's cloak would not get wet. The Devil agreed and shape-shifted into a seal.

On the voyage, Sæmundr read the Book of Psalms from the Bible. Just before they reached the coast, Sæmundr struck the seal's head with the Good Book, making it sink and thereby wetting his cloak. So the Devil lost that bargain, and Sæmundr became the director of the school.

To avenge the insult, the Devil changed himself into a fly and hid under the skin of the milk in a bowl, hoping that Sæmundr would swallow him so that the Devil could kill him from inside. But Sæmundr noticed the fly, and he wrapped it in a bladder and put it on the altar while he celebrated Mass. It is believed that the Devil did not enjoy the experience. When Mass was over, Sæmundr released the fly.

Kalf Arnason, who studied at the Devil's school after Sæmundr had left, and who had promised himself to the Devil, was worried that he would eventually have to fulfil the pledge. He went to Sæmundr and asked his advice.

"You have some bull calves," said the scholar. "Name one of them Arni. Let the bull breed, and name its son Kalf, so its full name will be Kalf Arnason."

And a calf was what the Devil got when he came to collect the soul of Kalf Arnason, who died of natural causes at a ripe old age.

(Adapted from *Icelandic Legends*, Jón Árnason, 1862.)

Modern scholars believe that Sæmundr founded the school at Oddi. It was there that his grandson raised Snorri Sturlusson, author of the Prose Edda.

The Bridges at Soravilla and Oiartzun
Gipuzkoa, Basque Country

A stonecutter in Soravilla was trying to build a bridge over the Río Oria, but the river was in spate and kept destroying his work. He said aloud, "Only the demons of Hell will be able to help me build this bridge."

The Devil himself appeared and offered to have the bridge built before cock-crow the following morning, in exchange for the man's soul. The stonecutter agreed to the bargain, thinking that this was impossible. Immediately, 14,000 devils all named Micolás set to work, and construction progressed rapidly. The stonecutter began to worry that he might have to pay the price after all. Fortunately, a wise woman came to him and said, "Take some salt and put it up the backside of the cock. That will make it crow."

The stonecutter did what she suggested, and when the cock crowed long before break of day, all the 14,000 devils named Micolás stopped work and returned to Hell, leaving the bridge as it was.

However, the work had been finished with the exception of one stone. When the people of Soravilla woke up in the morning and saw the new bridge, they noticed the gap. They fitted a stone into the waiting space, but by the following morning it had disappeared. Several times they put a stone in the hole, and each time it was gone the next day. Finally they gave up and left the space empty.

In 1988, Micaela Labaien Lasarte, aged 74, of Leiza gave that account to Juan Garmendia Larrañaga, who published it in his 1995 book *Mitos y leyendas de los Vascos*. In 1996, Fermín Leizaola Calvo, President of the Department of Ethnology at the Aranzadi Society of Sciences in San Sebastián, took me on an excursion to stone circles and dolmens in the nearby hills of Gipuzkoa. On our way back to San Sebastián, we stopped in the village of Oiartzun, not far from Soravilla. He showed me a bridge across the Río Oiartzun that had a stone missing and told me the same story about that bridge.

In 2016, I was telling stories in language schools in two towns on the Río Oria and had the opportunity to visit Soravilla. After several days of constant rain, the river was in spate, and I could see how difficult it would have been for the stonecutter to build a bridge without infernal aid. Unfortunately, the present utilitarian and unattractive bridge is made of concrete, and so there is no empty space where the last stone should be. It is obviously not the one in the story. However, I have photos of the bridge in Oiartzun from my 1996 visit (see back cover), and they clearly show the hole where the stone refused to stay: proof that the Oiartzun story, at least, is true.

Perurimá Saves the Holy Family
Paraguay

Perurimá was sitting outside his house one morning when he saw a man leading a burro that carried a young woman and a baby. They were moving quickly. As they came nearer he noticed haloes around their heads and knew that they were the Holy Family.

"Why are you in such a hurry?" he asked. "Why don't you stop here and rest?"

Joseph said, "We're on our way to Egypt to escape the Devil. He wants to kill our Child."

They passed on, and when they were out of sight around a bend in the road, Perú took some cold grey ashes from the fire and sprinkled them over the hoof prints of the burro. Soon the Devil arrived on a fine, fast horse.

"Did you happen to see a man with a young woman and a child pass by here?" he asked. "They were riding a burro."

"Oh, yes, I remember, but it was such a long time ago, I don't think you'll catch up with them."

"That's impossible. I was right behind them."

"Well, if you don't believe me, come over here and I'll show you the hoof prints of the burro."

The Devil dismounted and went to look.

"See?" said Perú. "They're so old they're already covered in dust."

The Devil gave up the chase, and the Holy Family was saved.

(*Aventuras*)

More adventures of Perurimá are in the Latin American Tricksters section.

Animals

"One of India's most influential contributions to world literature, *The Panchatantra* (also spelled *Pañcatantra* or *Pañca-tantra*) consists of five books of animal fables and magic tales (some 87 stories in all) that were compiled in their current form between the third and fifth centuries AD. It is believed that even then the stories were already ancient. The tales' self-proclaimed purpose is to educate the sons of royalty."

(D. L. Ashliman, editor and translator of the comprehensive and useful Folklore and Mythology Electronic Texts website.)

The Lion and the Hare
India, *The Panchatantra*

The lion of the forest, Bhâsuraka the Heroic, was killing the animals indiscriminately – not only to eat but also to show that he could. He killed many more than he needed for food, because he was a bully.

The animals went to him and said, "If you continue to slaughter us, there will be no animals left for you to eat. We have a suggestion. We will select one animal by lottery to come to you at noon each day for you to eat, if you agree to leave the rest of us alone."

Bhâsuraka agreed, and each day one animal presented itself at his den for his dinner. Then one day the lot fell on the hare. Though among the swiftest of foot, he dragged his feet on his way to the lion's den, trying to come up with a plan to save himself. But he was also swift of thought, and when he came across a well, he got an idea. It was several hours past noon when he arrived for his appointment with the lion. Bhâsuraka was as angry as he was hungry.

"You are late, hare. You have broken our agreement, and because of that I'm going to kill all the animals in the forest tomorrow."

"It's not my fault, sire, nor the fault of the other animals of the forest. Well, except one."

"Which one has made you late? I'll go and kill him after I eat you."

"I'm not sure you can do that, sire. He's a lion, and he's bigger than you."

"Another lion in this forest?"

"Yes, sire. He caught me on my way here and said he was going to eat me. I told him if he did that he would have to answer to you, because all the animals in this forest belong to you."

"And what did he say to that? I see he let you go."

"He let me go, sire, to bring you a message."

"What message?"

"He orders you to come to him so you both can decide who is the king of this forest."

"He orders me?"

"Yes, sire. He told me to show you where his castle is."

"His castle? He dares to build a castle in my forest? And sends me orders? Take me to his castle at once. I'm hungry enough to eat a lion."

The hare led Bhâsuraka to the well and said, "That's the lion's castle. Look and see if he's inside."

Bhâsuraka peered into the well and saw his reflection, thinking it was the other lion. He roared his loudest roar in challenge. Amplified by the stone walls of the well, the roar came back to him twice as loud.

"I'll teach you to build castles in my forest and send me orders," he growled, and he dived into the well, never to come back out.

K1715.1. Weak animal shows strong his own reflection and frightens him. Tells him that this animal is threatening to kill him. Usually hare and lion. (Africa, African-American, Tibet, Pakistan, Malaya)

The Goat and the Lion
India, *The Panchatantra*

The goat, according to the Hindu [Panchatantra] tale, took shelter during a storm in the den of a lion; when he saw no chance of escape, he terrified the king of the beasts by boasting of a celestial origin, and telling him he had been condemned before he could return to Heaven to eat ten elephants, ten tigers, and ten lions. He had, he said, eaten every kind of animal but the lion; and saying this, he marched up to the astonished monster, who fled by a back way from his den. The lion in his flight met a fox, and described to him the appearance of the goat (an animal he had never seen before), his horns, his strange beard, and above all, his boasting language. The fox laughed, and told his majesty how he had been tricked. They went back together, and met the goat at the entrance of the den. The latter at once saw his danger, but his wits did not forsake him. "What conduct is this, you scoundrel?" said he to the fox: "I commanded you to get ten lions, and here you have only brought me one;" so saying, he advanced boldly, and the lion, again frightened by his words and actions, fled in terror, allowing the goat to return quietly to his home.

(Verbatim from *Sketches of Persia*, John Malcolm, 1861. Malcolm told this tale to Hajee Hoosein in response to the Hajee's telling him the story of Ameen and the Ghoul.)

The Monkey's Heart
India, *The Panchatantra*

Monkey lived in a fruit tree next to the river. One day, Crocodile came close to the bank to watch him eat. Monkey noticed him and said, "You are welcome to the feast, Crocodile, for it is said, 'He is blessed who feeds a guest.'"

Crocodile couldn't climb into the tree, so Monkey threw fruits down to him. They became friends, and Monkey continued to share the fruits of the tree with Crocodile. Crocodile took some of the fruits to his home on the other side of the river and shared them with his wife.

"Where do you get these lovely sweet fruits?" she asked him one day.

"I have a new friend, Monkey, who throws them down from a tree."

"If Monkey eats these fruits all the time," she said, "he must be very sweet inside, and his heart must be the sweetest part of him. I would like to eat his heart."

Crocodile was shocked.

"That would be highly improper. He's my friend. He's like family. It is said, 'When a new friend you discover, treat him as you would a brother.'"

"I don't care about that. I think your heart is so full of your love for your new friend that you don't have any room in it for me. I can't live if you don't get that monkey's heart for me."

Crocodile saw that he would have to do what his wife wanted if he wanted peace in the house. He swam slowly on his way to meet Monkey the next day, working out a plan to get his friend's heart.

"Friend Crocodile, you're late. Why do you look so sad?"

"My wife told me that I have been very ungrateful to you for your generosity. She said I should have invited you home for dinner long ago, and she invites you to come and eat with us today."

"That is kind of her, and proper, for it is said, 'Friendship never ends, when friends share with friends.' But you live on the other side of the river. How will I get there?"

"Climb onto my back and I'll carry you."

Monkey jumped onto Crocodile's back and hung on tight. Halfway across the river, too far for Monkey to jump to safety, Crocodile thought it was safe to tell him the truth.

"Friend Monkey, I have to admit that my wife didn't really invite you to dinner, or not the kind of dinner you might expect."

"What do you mean?"

"My wife feels that since you eat sweet fruits all the time, your heart must be even sweeter, and she wants to eat your heart."

"And you agreed to that?"

"Not at first, but she thinks I love you more than I love her, and if I don't do what she wants she'll be impossible to live with. You know how wives are."

Monkey didn't, because he wasn't married, but he could imagine. He thought fast.

"But friend Crocodile, I'd be happy to give her my heart. You should have told me before we started across the river. I never carry my heart with me. You've seen how I leap and swing through the trees – my heart would fall out. I always leave it in my nest in the tree, where it's safe. Turn around and let's go back so I can get it for you."

"Oh, friend Monkey, thank you for being as generous with your heart as you are with the fruit."

Crocodile turned around and let Monkey jump off on the bank near his tree. Monkey scrambled up the tree, ate some fruit, and lay down for a nap. Crocodile waited and waited, and finally he called out, "Friend Monkey, have you found your heart yet? My wife will be getting impatient."

"Friendless Crocodile, tell your heartless wife that I have decided I need my heart more than she does. And I recommend that both of you contemplate the second part of that first proverb I quoted: 'Angels will desert the nest that unkindly treats a guest.'"

All versions I have seen feature a monkey, most have a crocodile as the antagonist, one has a shark. In some, an important personage is ill, and only the heart or liver or gizzard of a monkey will cure them. This type includes one of the Brer Rabbit tales. One version uses the motif: "K561.3. Crocodile persuaded to open his mouth. When he does, he shuts his eyes automatically and monkey escapes."

K544. Escape by alleged possession of external soul. Monkey caught for his heart (as remedy) makes his captor believe that he has left his heart at home.

The Monkey and the Turtle
by Mabel Cook Cole (1916)
Ilocano, Philippines

A monkey, looking very sad and dejected, was walking along the bank of the river one day when he met a turtle.

"How are you?" asked the turtle, noticing that he looked sad.

The monkey replied, "Oh, my friend, I am very hungry. The squash of Mr. Farmer were all taken by the other monkeys, and now I am about to die from want of food."

"Do not be discouraged," said the turtle; "take a bolo [machete] and follow me and we will steal some banana plants."

So they walked along together until they found some nice plants which they dug up, and then they looked for a place to set them. Finally the monkey climbed a tree and planted his in it, but as the turtle could not climb he dug a hole in the ground and set his there.

When their work was finished they went away, planning what they should do with their crop. The monkey said:

"When my tree bears fruit, I shall sell it and have a great deal of money."

And the turtle said: "When my tree bears fruit, I shall sell it and buy three varas [metres] of cloth to wear in place of this cracked shell."

A few weeks later they went back to the place to see their plants and found that that of the monkey was dead, for its roots had had no soil in the tree, but that of the turtle was tall and bearing fruit.

"I will climb to the top so that we can get the fruit," said the monkey. And he sprang up the tree, leaving the poor turtle on the ground alone.

"Please give me some to eat," called the turtle, but the monkey threw him only a green one and ate all the ripe ones himself.

When he had eaten all the good bananas, the monkey stretched his arms around the tree and went to sleep. The turtle, seeing this, was very angry and considered how he might punish the thief. Having decided on a scheme, he gathered some sharp bamboo which he stuck all around under the tree, and then he exclaimed:

"Crocodile is coming! Crocodile is coming!"

The monkey was so startled at the cry that he fell upon the sharp bamboo and was killed.

Then the turtle cut the dead monkey into pieces, put salt on it, and dried it in the sun. The next day, he went to the mountains and sold his meat to other monkeys who gladly gave him squash in return. As he was leaving them he called back:

"Lazy fellows, you are now eating your own body; you are now eating your own body."

Then the monkeys ran and caught him and carried him to their own home.

"Let us take a hatchet," said one old monkey, "and cut him into very small pieces."

But the turtle laughed and said: "That is just what I like. I have been struck with a hatchet many times. Do you not see the black scars on my shell?"

Then one of the other monkeys said: "Let us throw him into the water."

At this the turtle cried and begged them to spare his life, but they paid no heed to his pleadings and threw him into the water. He sank to the bottom, but very soon came up with a lobster. The monkeys were greatly surprised at this and begged him to tell them how to catch lobsters.

"I tied one end of a string around my waist," said the turtle. "To the other end of the string I tied a stone so that I would sink."

The monkeys immediately tied strings around themselves as the turtle said, and when all was ready they plunged into the water never to come up again.

And to this day monkeys do not like to eat meat, because they remember the ancient story.

Source author's note

This tale told by the Ilocano is well known among both the Christianized and the wild tribes of the Philippines, and also in Borneo and Java. However, the Ilocano is the only version, so far as known, which has the explanatory element: the reason is given here why monkeys do not eat meat. The turtle is accredited with extraordinary sagacity and cunning. It is another example of the type of tale showing the victory of the weak and cunning over the strong but stupid.

From *Philippine Folk Tales*, compiled and annotated by Mabel Cook Cole, McClurg, Chicago, 1916. Because this story is out of copyright and in the public domain – belongs to everyone and no one – I have reproduced it here verbatim except for inserting "[machete]" and "[metres]".

The Uncle Remus "Tar Baby" story is the best known version of this wide-spread tale.

K581.2. Briar-patch punishment for rabbit. By expressing horror of being thrown into the briar patch he induces his captor into doing so. He runs off.

K584. Throwing the thief over the fence. Thief, surprised at theft says: "Do your worst, only don't throw me over the fence." When thrown over, he escapes.

K581. Animal "punished" by being placed in favourite environment.

K581.1. Drowning punishment for turtle (eel, crab). By expressing horror of drowning, he induces his captor to throw him into the water – his home.

Anansi and the Pot of Wisdom
Africa

Anansi (Spider) is to Africa what Coyote is to North American natives: a demi-god, often in human form, who helps the Creator, and a trickster whose selfish tricks tend to backfire. The usual pronunciation sounds like "Aunt Nancy", which is why that is one of his names in African-American lore, but I have heard "ah-nah-SEE" from a Jamaican. Anansi's adventures became widely known through his non-divine cousin Brer Rabbit in the 1946 Disney film *Song of the South*, based on Uncle Remus stories collected from oral tradition by Joel Chandler Harris and published individually from 1879 and eventually in nine books.

One day, Anansi decided to collect all the wisdom of the world into one pot, so that only he could have it. He needed to put the pot in a place where no one else could reach it, so he hung the pot from his neck and started to climb the highest tree in the forest. But the pot swinging in front of him kept getting in the way, and soon for each foot he climbed up he was sliding two feet down.

His son was watching, and he said, "Daddy, why don't you swing the pot around so it's behind you and won't interfere with your climbing?"

"I was just about to do that," Anansi grumbled, embarrassed that he hadn't thought of it himself.

But in swinging the pot around to his back, he dropped it, and it smashed to pieces on the ground. The wisdom flowed down to the river, and from there out to the sea and all around the world. That is why everyone on earth has a bit of wisdom, but no one has all of it.

Some of that wisdom must have splashed onto Anansi, though, because as he climbed down the tree he said, "It wasn't right for me to try to keep all the wisdom, because look: even a child could see that I was doing it all wrong."

The Eagle and the Dung Beetle
Greece/Aesop

Dung beetles – the sacred scarabs in Egyptian tradition – are found everywhere on the planet except Antarctica. David Attenborough has described them as "a highly efficient waste disposal service". They gather dung and pack it into a ball, which they roll to a hidden cache for food or into a brooding chamber. They mate underground, and the female lays her eggs in a dung ball in the brooding chamber.

A hare was being chased by an eagle. Desperate, he appealed for help to a dung beetle. The tiny beetle confronted the eagle and said, "This hare is under my protection, and I ask you in the name of Zeus, patron of eagles, to honour it."

The eagle ignored the beetle and killed and ate the hare. Seeking revenge for the death of the hare and the insult to his honour, the beetle discovered where the eagle had her nest.

The next time the eagle laid eggs, the beetle flew up to her nest and pushed the eggs out so that they smashed on the ground. Outraged at the destruction of her eggs, the eagle flew to Zeus and asked him to provide a safe place to lay her eggs. Zeus told her that she could lay them in his lap. When the beetle found out, he gathered a big ball of dung and, soaring high, dropped it in Zeus's lap.

Forgetting about the eggs, Zeus sprang up to get rid of the dung, and the eggs fell to the ground.

Zeus was angry with the beetle, but the beetle explained that the eagle had not only violated his protection of the hare but also defied his invocation of the name of Zeus. The god solved the problem by changing the beetle's breeding season so that it would be kept busy underground minding its young during the time the eagle laid her eggs.

This story is referenced in Aristophanes' 420 BC play *Peace*. Trygaeus is going to visit Olympus, and he tells his little daughter that he will ride on the back of a gigantic dung beetle.

"But what an idea, papa, to harness a beetle to fly to the gods on."

He explains: "We see from Aesop's fables that they alone can fly to the abode of the Immortals."

"Father, that's a tale nobody can believe, that such a smelly creature can have gone to the gods."

"It went to have vengeance on the eagle and break its eggs."

Abidoo
Philippines

Monkey, Deer and Turtle made their living by fishing. One night, a monster named Abidoo came and stole all the fish they had caught that day. So the next night, Monkey kept watch, but he was not strong enough to prevent Abidoo stealing the fish. The following night, Deer kept watch, but Abidoo got the fish anyway.

The third night it was Turtle's turn for guard duty. She was just an ordinary small turtle, not a big tortoise, and she knew that she would have to use her brain, so she came up with a plan. She told Monkey and Deer to stay nearby, and she told Deer what to do when she whistled.

Abidoo had come at midnight the previous three nights, so before that time Turtle started making a rope from sisal, with one end of it tied to a tree. When Abidoo arrived to steal the fish, Turtle began braiding the rope frantically. Abidoo noticed and said, "Turtle, what are you doing?"

Turtle said, "Typhoon is coming. Please tie me to this tree with the rope so he can't blow me away and kill me. Then you can take all the fish you want."

When Abidoo heard that, he got scared.

"No. *You* tie *me* to the tree or *I'll* kill you."

So Turtle tied Abidoo to the tree, and when she pulled the knot tight she stepped away and whistled.

"What's that sound?" said Abidoo.

"It's Typhoon. He's coming. Close your eyes. He's horrible."

Abidoo closed his eyes, shivering and shaking as he heard the sound of hooves galloping closer and closer, until, WHAM! Deer butted him in the stomach, knocking the wind out of him and leaving him unconscious.

Monkey, Deer and Turtle went home and slept until daylight. When they returned to the tree where Turtle had tied Abidoo, they found that he had managed to untie the knot and escape, but he never came back to steal their fish again.

K713.1.1. Animal allows himself to be tied so as to avoid being carried off by storm.

King of the Birds
United States

Grandma told me about the bat who hid himself on top of the eagle's back, screaming, "I can fly higher than any other bird." That was true enough; even the eagle couldn't fly higher than somebody who was sitting on top of him. As a punishment the other birds grounded the bat and put him in a mouse hole. There he fell in love with a lady mouse. That is why bats now are half mouse and half bird.

(From *Lame Deer: Seeker of Visions*.)

A series of photos on the National Geographic website published on 2 July 2015 shows a crow landing on the back of a bald eagle in flight and perching there briefly before flying away. Commentators say the crow was about to attack the eagle, probably to protect its territory, but then decided not to. Or perhaps the eagle flew away from the crow's territory.

Or was it a competition to decide who would be king of the birds?

B236.0.1. Animal king chosen as result of a contest.

B242.1.2. Wren king of birds. Wins contest for kingship.

The Caged Bird

A singing bird lived in a cage in the palace. He was the favourite of the princess. One day he heard that the princess was going to visit a king in the bird's home country, where he and his brother had been captured. His brother lived in a cage in the palace of that king.

"Please," he said to the princess, "when you visit the king, tell my brother, who lives with him, where I am and what I am doing."

The princess said that she would. When she returned, the bird asked if she had given the message to his brother. She said she had.

"What was his reaction?"

"He fell down dead."

"Oh," said the bird, and he fell to the floor of his cage with his legs in the air.

When the princess saw that, she called one of her servants.

"This bird has died. Throw his body out the window."

The servant did that, and the bird soared into the air and flew to his home country to be reunited with his brother.

(I got this tale from Israeli storyteller Lois Tzur.)

J1118. Clever bird.

How a Dog Brought Rice to Humans
Lisu Tribe, Thailand

After Brahma created the world and people, he got lazy and ignored them. The people fed themselves by hunting and gathering, but they weren't very good hunters, and they couldn't thrive on the roots and berries they gathered. In fact, they were weak and starving.

Vishnu took pity on them. He told the people that the giants grew rice in their land beyond the mountains, and if the people could only find a way to steal some – for the giants hoarded it selfishly, and Vishnu understood that it was good for people to work for their food – they could plant it and prosper. But there was a problem. The mountains were too high to climb. The only way in to the giants' country was through a tunnel in the back of a certain cave, and the tunnel was too narrow for even the smallest of the people to fit.

Dogs had already been created – some say that happened even before humans appeared in the world – and were at least as clever and intelligent as the people, and certainly more experienced in solving problems. So the people selected a small dog and explained that they needed him to go through the tunnel and bring back some rice seeds. They trusted him to figure out how to accomplish the task.

The dog understood. He went through the tunnel and found the place where the giants were drying the rice and kept other types of food. There was bread, salt, meat, and jars of honey, all guarded by a huge dozing giant. It occurred to the dog that even if he could get some of the rice, he had no way to carry it back to the people; he had no sack or other container, and even if he did, it wouldn't fit through the tunnel. He worked out a plan.

He went to the giant and woke him up by barking. The giant grabbed a club and tried to hit the dog, but the dog was quick and agile, and he moved to stand in front of the jars of honey and barked defiantly. The giant swung his club, the dog jumped aside, and the club smashed the

85

honey jars. The dog rolled in the honey and then the pile of rice seeds, which stuck to the honey, and made his way to the tunnel and home to the people.

In another version, God had rice growing on the far side of a lake. The people didn't know how to swim, and they sent a dog across. He rolled in the seeds and brought them back stuck to his wet fur.

It is still a custom among the Lisu to share their rice-based meals with dogs in gratitude for the heroism of the one who saved the people from starvation.

A522.1.1. Dog as culture hero.

A1705. Animals created to serve man.

A2493.4. Friendship between man and dog.

Kalulu
Zambia

"When thief thief thief, God laugh." Africa

"Kalulu" is the word for "hare" in Zambia and some other African countries, but it is often translated as "rabbit", like his African-American cousin Brer Rabbit. Because of his constant trickery, he was banished to the moon, where you can see him on a clear full-moon night.

On a day when all the other animals had left their homes to work, Kalulu, who preferred playing – and especially playing tricks – made a lasso out of a vine and brought the nest of Buzzard down to the ground. One of the eggs fell out, and Kalulu took it to his warren.

When the animals returned from work, Buzzard called to the others and said, "Someone has stolen one of my eggs."

The wise Elephant said, "Leave the nest on the ground. Let Caracal keep watch tomorrow to catch the thief if he returns to take the other eggs."

Kalulu was listening. He knew that Caracal, the red lynx, was a wily and feared hunter, but he had a plan. While everyone else was asleep, he set the loop of his lasso next to Buzzard's nest and covered it with dirt, and ran the vine over a branch.

When the other animals went to work in the morning, Caracal hid in the bushes. Kalulu rustled some leaves behind a tree near the nest. Caracal's big ears picked up the sound, and he thought it was the thief. With a mighty leap he landed next to the nest – and in the middle of the lasso loop. Kalulu tripped the vine, and the loop tightened on Caracal's foot to pull him up and leave him dangling in the air

"Help," called Caracal, but the other animals were too far away to hear him.

While the lynx struggled helplessly, Kalulu snatched another egg and took it home.

When the others returned, they set Caracal free, but Buzzard complained, "The thief has taken another egg."

They appointed Baboon to guard the nest the following day, but the same thing happened to him and to Leopard the day after that. Two more eggs were missing, and there was only one left.

"Who will guard the last egg tomorrow?" Elephant asked.

"I will," said young Tortoise.

"You? But Caracal and Baboon and Leopard all failed, and they're older and much more experienced than you. And you're scarcely bigger than one of Buzzard's eggs. How do you think you can catch the thief?"

"I have a plan," said Tortoise, who had been watching and thinking. When the others went to sleep, he crawled into Buzzard's nest. It had also occurred to him that he was only slightly bigger than the remaining egg and not much different in colour.

When the animals had left in the morning, Tortoise heard leaves rustle near the nest, but he kept his head and feet inside his shell. He heard the rustling again, but still didn't move.

Kalulu was puzzled. Where was Tortoise? Why didn't he come running to be caught in the lasso? He went to the nest and saw not one but two eggs. He thought he had miscounted or hadn't noticed the other egg before. He started to pick up the larger one, but Tortoise snaked his head out of his shell and clamped his jaws on Kalulu's paw.

"Let me go," he said. "I'll share the other eggs with you. What do you say to that?"

Tortoise said nothing. He had heard the old story of the Talkative Tortoise who wanted to fly. Two swans held a stick between them and told him to grab it in his mouth but to remember not to speak. They flew high with him, and he was so delighted that he began to say, "Oh, what a beautiful view." But he got no further than opening his mouth to say "Oh" and fell to the ground, cracking his shell.

So Tortoise kept his mouth shut and held on to Kalulu's paw until the other animals returned and discovered who the thief was. They made him bring back Buzzard's other eggs, and then they strung him up with his own lasso and left him swinging until the following day. They only let him go free when he promised not to steal any more eggs.

But they neglected to make him promise not to play any more tricks.

Kalulu wasn't really bad. In fact, some of his tricks were actually beneficial to someone besides himself. One example is the time he saved a village from a python and won the hand of a princess.

The python, which had two mouths and was as big as a tree, had taken up residence in a tree in the middle of the village. It came down at night and ate small animals, then bigger animals. The people were afraid it was going to start eating their children. Many men tried to kill it but failed. Some suggested that the tree be cut down, but it was sacred, so that was not an option.

Finally, in desperation, the chief spread word that anyone who managed to kill the python could marry his daughter, the princess. (She was not a real princess, but she was so charming and intelligent and beautiful that everyone called her Princess.)

Kalulu heard about this, and he came to the village leading a goat and a dog, with hay in one hand and meat in the other. He asked the chief to repeat his offer. The chief said, "If you kill the python, you can marry the princess."

Kalulu took the dog and the goat to the tree where the python was lurking and told everyone to step back. Then he tied the goat to one stake and the dog to another. He placed the hay in front of the dog and said, "Eat." He placed the meat in front of the goat and said, "Eat." Not surprisingly, the dog refused to eat the hay, and the goat refused to eat the meat. The people wondered at the stupidity of Kalulu. Even the most foolish among them would not try to feed meat to a goat and hay to a dog.

Kalulu kicked the dog and the goat and beat them with a stick, shouting, "Eat, eat." They still didn't eat.

"These animals refuse to obey me. I'm going to have to kill them. Bring me an axe."

Some of the villagers said, "How is killing them going to help us solve our problem?"

"Never mind that," said Kalulu. "Bring me an axe."

So they brought an axe and handed it to him.

"Now, goat and dog, if you don't eat what I put in front of you, I'm going to chop off your heads."

And he raised the axe.

The python enjoyed being able to terrorize humans. He was old and experienced in the world, and conceit made him arrogant. So full of a sense of self-importance was he, that he couldn't bear to watch the silliness of the nitwit hare without offering his sage advice. He slithered down the tree and began to place the meat in front of the dog and the hay in front of the goat.

As he was busy doing this, Kalulu brought the axe down on his neck, killing him.

So Kalulu married the princess, and the chief built them a new hut and supplied them and their family with food for the rest of their lives.

(Adapted from *Folk Tales of Zambia*, Chiman L. Vyas, 1974.)

The Farmer and the Wolf and the Three Judges
Galicia, Spain

A farmer was walking along a road on his way to work a field, when he saw that there had been a flood, and a wolf was trapped under earth and stones with only his head showing. When the wolf saw the man, he said, "Help me out of here or I'll die."

The man said, "I'd be happy to do that, but I'm afraid you'd eat me once you're free."

"I'd never do that to someone who saved my life."

"Well, if I could be sure of that ... but it will take a lot of effort on my part to release you."

"I promise I won't eat you – wolf's honour."

So the man took the mattock off his shoulder and dug and dug until finally the wolf was free.

"Thanks for that," said the wolf, "but now I'm obliged to eat you."

"Well, if that's the way it is. But since I did you a favour, you owe me a favour."

"What is the favour you want?"

"To ask three judges their opinion. If they all agree that you have a right to eat me, I'll accept that."

"Fair enough, but let's hurry. My stomach is growling from hunger."

They walked along the road and soon came upon an old nag of a horse.

"Good day, Mister Horse," said the wolf. "We'd like your opinion on a matter in dispute."

He explained the case, and the horse said, "I say eat him.

"When I was young, my master was a member of the king's troop, and he rode me in parades. At home they fed me brome and alfalfa, rubbed me down after work and took good care of me. Then one day my mistress was riding me to the mill, and I fell and broke my teeth. When we got home I heard her say to my master, 'We have to get rid of that horse. I was nearly killed when he stumbled and I fell off. Take him to the mountains and let the wolves eat him.'

"And so they did and here I am – no respect, no teeth to eat with, dying. I say eat the man."

"Well," said the wolf to the man with a nasty laugh, "things seem to be going my way, don't you think?"

"We'll see."

They walked until they met an old dog. This time the man explained the dispute.

"I can't say one way or the other," said the dog. "When I was young I worked the stock with my master and guarded his house and played with his children. Now I am old and can't see well enough to work the stock and can't hear well enough to guard the house. They wanted to drown me, so I ran away."

"It looks like I'm going to eat you," said the wolf to the man. "They're all in agreement."

"Not so fast. We still need a third opinion."

So they walked until they spied a fox sitting high on an outcrop.

"What are you doing here, wolf?" the fox called out. "I don't think much of the company you're keeping."

"We need your opinion to settle a dispute," said the man. The fox climbed down from the rock and whispered in the man's ear, "Do you have lambs and chickens?"

"Yes. Lots of them."

"Then relax and let me handle this."

The fox moved away from the man and said, "Tell me what the disagreement is about."

The man explained that the wolf was trapped under stones and earth after a flood and promised not to eat him if he would rescue him, but now thinks he has a right to eat him.

"It sounds very complicated," said the fox. "I can't make a decision unless I see the whole situation. Take me to the place where this happened."

They took him there, but the fox said, "I still don't understand. Where exactly was the man and where exactly was the wolf?"

So the wolf sat exactly on the spot where he had been buried, and the man stood in the road.

"But you can move freely," said the fox to the wolf.

"I was buried up to my neck at the time."

"Show me."

The wolf and the man dug and scraped away the stones and earth until there was a hole deep enough for the wolf to sit in with his head just above the level of the ground. Then the man scraped the earth and stones into the hole and around the wolf so only his head was showing.

"Is that the way you were?"

"Yes. Now get me out of here or I'll die."

"My decision is that you should stay there forever for breaking your promise."

The man and the fox walked away from the wolf, the man on the road and the fox taking a parallel path along the side of the hill.

"Come home with me," said the man, "and you can feast on lambs and chickens."

"Bring them here to me," said the fox, jumping onto the top of a wall.

The man went home and said to his wife, "Put two lambs and two chickens in a sack."

"What for?"

"To give to a fox that saved me from being eaten by a wolf."

"Ha. Put two dogs in a sack and take them to the fox."

The man did that, and when he arrived at the wall where the fox was waiting, he said, "I'll bring the lambs and chickens up to you."

"No. Leave them there."

The man opened the sack and let the dogs out. They chased the fox over hill and dale, through briars and bushes, until finally he managed to escape. He was bleeding all over and his paws were full of thorns.

"Oh, my feet, oh, my feet!
All the world does nothing but cheat."

J1172.3. Ungrateful animal returned to captivity.
W154.2.1. Rescued animal threatens rescuer.
K235.1. Fox is promised chickens: is driven off by dogs.
W154.2.2. Man ungrateful for rescue by animal.
(Grateful beasts and thankless man – *The Panchatantra*)

You can't trust anyone
China

All the country people knew that the tiger could shape-shift into an old woman. So when a woman had to leave her children alone for a few days while she visited her dying father on the other side of the mountains, she warned her daughter, who was seven, and her son, who was five, not to open the door to anyone while she was away. They assured her they wouldn't.

Late in the afternoon, they heard a knock at the door. They kept quiet.

"Are you going to leave me outside here all night?" came a woman's voice.

The children hugged each other in fear and remained silent.

"What's the matter? Are you afraid? Don't you remember your auntie?"

"We don't have an aunt," the girl called out.

"I'm your great-aunt, the sister of your grandmother who lives on the other side of the mountains."

Aunt Tiger – for that's who she was – pushed some rice cakes covered with honey under the door.

"Well, if you won't let me in," the voice continued, "at least eat these cakes that your grandmother and I baked so I won't have to carry them back home."

"Don't go," said the children together, and they opened the door.

93

"You're very prudent," said Aunt Tiger when she was seated on the best chair in the house. "It's good that you're careful, because two children would make an appetizing dish for a certain class of beast."

The children smiled. The woman knew lots of games, and she played with them and imitated the sounds of wild animals for their amusement until finally she yawned and said, "I'm getting sleepy. It's time for me to go to bed."

"You can sleep in our mother's bed. It's big and comfortable so you can rest well."

"I'm scared of the dark. Will you share the bed with me so I won't be afraid?"

They got into the bed, Aunt Tiger in the middle, the boy next to the wall, and the girl on the outside. When the girl was asleep, Aunt Tiger took a handful of sleep-making herbs and anaesthetized the boy with them. Then she pulled off his thumb and began to eat it. She was sucking and slurping so loudly that the girl woke up.

"What are you eating, Auntie? Can you give me some? I'm hungry."

Aunt Tiger tore off one of the boy's little fingers and gave it to the girl, who immediately understood what was happening. She said nothing, but she made sucking and slurping sounds with her mouth. Then she pretended to fall asleep. After a few minutes, she tried to get out of bed, but Aunt Tiger held her with a claw.

"Trying to escape, are you? You'd like to wake up the men of the village so they can kill me, but I won't let you."

"What are you talking about? I just want to go to the toilet. I think those rice cakes didn't agree with my stomach."

"I don't trust you."

"Look, tie this rope around my waist, and that way you can check on my movements."

Aunt Tiger agreed, but instead of going to the toilet, the girl went out to the garden and tied the end of the rope around a tree. Then she went into the kitchen and boiled a pot of oil.

"What's taking you so long? You're not preparing any tricks, are you?"

The voice of Aunt Tiger sounded sleepy, for the anaesthetic herbs from the boy's thumb were having their effect on her. The girl climbed the tree with the pot of boiling oil and sat with it in the branches. She called out:

"Auntie, auntie, do you know where I am?"

Aunt Tiger followed the rope to the tree. When she looked up, the girl poured the boiling oil straight into her face. With a shriek and a howl of agony, Aunt Tiger ran out of the village, never to return, screaming, "Why did I trust a human cub? You can't trust anyone!"

The noise woke up the villagers, and they came to see what had happened. When the girl told her story, they didn't believe her.

"A girl destroyed a tiger? Impossible. You just had a nightmare."

But when she took some of the tiger's blood from below the tree and rubbed it on her brother's hand, and a new thumb and little finger grew, they believed. And they understood the meaning of the lament that came from a distance:

"You can't trust anyone!"

Humans

Ameen and the Ghoul
Persia (Iran)

The ancient city of Isfahan, in its days of glory one of the largest cities in the world, was twice the capital of Persia. It nestles in a mile-high (1590m) north-south fertile plain bordered to the east and west by the double folds of the dry and desolate Zagros Mountain range, which rises to 14,921 feet (4548m). Isfahan's historical prominence is largely due to its location as the hub of major north-south and east-west trade routes, as well as the ethnic, cultural and religious diversity of its inhabitants.

The antiquity and cosmopolitan nature of such a geographically isolated and commercially important city is bound to attract a mystique of mystery and the occult. One example is "the magic rope of Isfahan" used by the hero in the 1924 Douglas Fairbanks film *The Thief of Bagdad*. Another is the tradition that ghouls roam the rocky surrounding wastelands. A ghoul (Arabic *ghūl*) is a demon that lurks in graveyards and uninhabited places and kills and devours humans or feeds on recently deceased corpses. It can assume human shape, frequently that of the person it has most recently eaten.

Ameen Beg, a merchant and a native of Isfahan, grew up listening to the elders tell terrifying stories about the demons and denizens of the dark places outside the city walls, and he was well acquainted with the nature and habits of ghouls. So when he found it necessary one night to travel alone through the Valley of the Angel of Death, he put a raw egg and a lump of salt in his pocket and set out with confidence and a sense of adventure.

Once he was away from the lights of the city and into the foothills of the Zagros, it wasn't long before he heard a familiar voice from among the rocks:

96

"Hello, Ameen Beg. It's your old friend Kereem. You are going the wrong way. Come here to me before you get lost."

Ameen knew from the old stories that ghouls can take on the appearance of friends and imitate their voices, and since he had just bade farewell to Kereem in Isfahan, he had no doubt that a ghoul had discovered him. But he loved a challenge, so he followed the sound of the voice until he met with the false Kereem.

"I know you're not Kereem, and I know what you are. The reason I came here is to find a ghoul."

The ghoul stared in surprise and said nothing.

"I have travelled all over the world," Ameen continued, "and I have never found any creature, human or animal, that was my equal in strength. But I haven't had the opportunity to match myself against a ghoul. So here I am and here you are."

"You don't look very strong," said the ghoul, eyeing him up and down.

"They all said that. Appearances can be deceptive. I'll give you proof."

He picked up a stone that was the same colour as the egg in his pocket and handed it to the ghoul.

"See if you can squeeze some liquid out of that."

The ghoul squeezed but no liquid came out. While the ghoul was distracted, Ameen took the egg out of his pocket and palmed it.

"It's impossible," said the ghoul, handing the stone back to Ameen. "It's as dry as ... as a stone."

"Watch this," said Ameen, squeezing the egg so it dribbled through his fingers. While the ghoul gazed in amazement, Ameen took the lump of salt out of his pocket. He selected a stone the colour of salt and held it up.

"I feel salt in this stone. See if you can crumble it and get the salt out."

The ghoul refused to try, so Ameen worked it around in the hand with the salt in it.

"Hold your hand out."

The ghoul did so, and Ameen crumbled the salt into its hand. The ghoul tasted it and looked at Ameen with respect and fear, remembering that the man had said he wanted to match strength with a ghoul.

"Good sir," it said, "my home is very nearby. Would you be kind enough to honour me by accepting a meal and accommodation for the night? Then you can resume your journey refreshed in the morning."

Ameen knew by experience that most humans find it difficult to lie, and they are easy to see through when they try. But he had learned from the elders' tales that ghouls were deceivers by nature. It would be safer to keep his enemy in front of him than to turn his back on it, so he said:

"I'd be delighted to accept your offer of hospitality, but I warn you – if you plan any trickery you will feel my displeasure."

The ghoul led the way through the boulders down a narrow defile to a large cave dimly lit by candles. It showed him into rooms off the main chamber, where Ameen saw skeletons and half-eaten remains of his host's victims and a hoard of the plunder it had taken from them. A merchant by nature and trade, Ameen quickly assessed the value of the gold, silver, jewellery, spices and rich cloths and calculated that here was a fortune ripe for the taking. To his main goal of survival he now added looting, which he preferred to think of as the liberation of ill-gotten goods. The ghoul picked up a bag of rice that could feed Ameen for two months.

"Will this be enough for your dinner?" it said.

"I ate that amount of rice and a whole sheep before I left Isfahan," said Ameen, "but I've worked up an appetite with the evening's walk, so I won't offend you by refusing that little bit."

"I know you humans like your food cooked. I'll get firewood while you use that bag to bring water to the fire pit from the stream."

The ghoul stomped off in the dark with an axe. The bag the ghoul had indicated was made of several cowhides stitched together. Ameen could barely drag it to the stream empty, and he knew that if he failed to fetch water his lack of the great strength he had boasted would be exposed to the ghoul. But the Isfahanees are renowned for their wit, and Ameen soon came up with a plan. He started to dig a channel from the stream to the fire pit and was still digging when the ghoul returned with an arm load of wood.

"What are you doing, man?" it shouted. "Where is the water to boil the rice?"

"To express my gratitude for your hospitality, I'm making a channel to bring the water from the stream to the fire pit, so in future you won't have to waste time and energy carrying it."

"I'll bring the water myself while you finish your project," the ghoul grumbled. It filled the bag at the stream and brought it to the fire pit.

After the meal, most of which Ameen managed to hide in his clothing, the ghoul made up a bed for him with a heap of pilfered cloths and robes and retired to the far side of the cave. As soon as Ameen heard its snores, he rose quietly and stuffed material into a long pillow to form a lumpy human-like shape in the bed and concealed himself in a dark corner. Shortly before sunrise, the ghoul quietly got out of bed – in its natural hideous form, which made Ameen shiver with fright – and picked up a club the size of a small tree. It padded silently to the bed that Ameen had vacated and struck a savage blow at the spot where Ameen's head would have been, then six more blows up and down the lumpy pillow.

Satisfied with its work, the ghoul went back to its own bed, while Ameen tiptoed back to his. As soon as the ghoul settled under its covers, Ameen called out, "My friend, I hope I don't wake you, but I thought I heard you moving. There is a fly or something that was batting its wings on my covers. Do you know what it is? It woke me up, and it's very annoying."

The ghoul said nothing, but ran as fast as it could out of the cave. Ameen found an old musket among the ghoul's purloined possessions and loaded it, in case the ghoul had second thoughts about its guest's might and invulnerability. He had noted the route by which the ghoul had led him to its cave, and as he made his way along the path he saw the ghoul coming toward him in the company of a fox. He knew the ghoul wasn't very bright, and he guessed that the fox had told it that it had been tricked. He aimed the musket at the fox and shot it through the head, killing it instantly.

"That's what happens to those who disobey my orders," he said to the ghoul. "I told that fox to bring me seven more ghouls so that I could chain them and take them to Isfahan to sell as slaves along with yourself."

The ghoul ran off, never to be seen again in the vicinity of Isfahan.

Ameen went home and organized a caravan of mules and wagons to collect the treasures in the cave. When he brought them back to Isfahan, he advertised that certain valuables had been found, and he would happily restore them to the rightful owners if they could accurately describe them. There were very few legitimate claims, of course, since most of the owners were dead. So Ameen became a very wealthy man.

K541. Escape by reporting oneself invulnerable and overawing captor.

K1766. Trickster's boasting scares his powerful opponent from contest.

K525.1. Substituted object left in bed while intended victim escapes.

K62. Contest in squeezing water from a stone. The ogre squeezes a stone; the trickster a cheese or egg.

K1741.3.1. Bluff: told to bring water in an ox skin, hero prepares to dig a canal.

K1715.2. Bluff: only one tiger; you promised ten. Child (or shepherd) calls out to the small hero (ape, hare) and makes the tiger (ogre) think that he is lucky to escape alive. (Goat and Lion in *The Panchatantra*)

This story is told by Hajee Hoosein, who described it as "a story that is well authenticated," in John Malcolm's *Sketches of Persia* (1861), which is probably the source of several subsequent publications. A children's version omits the scene where the fox is killed. After hearing the story from the Hajee, Malcolm tells him the tale of the Goat and the Lion; see that chapter in the Animals section.

The Birds of Cirencester
by Francis Bret Harte
(1836-1902)
England
(three of ten stanzas)

A. D. Five Hundred and Fifty-two,
The Saxon invaders – a terrible crew –
Had forced the lines of the Britons through;
And Cirencester, half mud and thatch,
Dry and crisp as a tinder match,
Was fiercely beleaguered by foes, who'd catch
At any device that could harry and rout
The folk that so boldly were holding out.

So they brought them some nets, which straightway
    they filled
With the swallows and martlets – the sweet birds who
    build
In the houses of man – all that innocent guild
Who sing at their labor on eaves and in thatch –
And they stuck on their feathers a rude lighted match
Made of resin and tow. Then they let them all go
To be free! As a child-like diversion? Ah, no!
To work Cirencester's red ruin and woe.

For straight to each nest they flew, in wild quest
Of their homes and their fledglings that they loved the
    best;
And straighter than arrow of Saxon e'er sped

They shot o'er the curving streets, high overhead,
Bringing fire and terror to roof tree and bed,
Till the town broke in flame, wherever they came,
To the Briton's red ruin, the Saxon's red shame!

K2351.1. Sparrows of Cirencester. Fire is attached to birds who fly in and set fire to a besieged city. (See Saints and Sieges section for the use of this trick in Russia. The name of the Gloucestershire town is pronounced "SIrencester," alternatively, "sisister" or "sister" and often simply "siren".)

The Black Pig's Dyke
Ireland

I've been telling this story for so long I have no idea where it came from. It's always a hit in schools. I introduce it by saying, "Do you want to hear a story about a *bad* teacher?"

The kids respond with an enthusiastic "Yes" and a guilty glance at the teacher, who – so far – has always taken it with a sense of humour.

The story explains the origins of (probably) defensive ditches all over Ireland, some up to ten feet deep, dated by archaeologists to about two thousand years ago.

A schoolmaster had the power to change people into animals by tapping them on the head with his magic wand. One day at the break, he changed the boys into hounds and the girls into hares, and the hounds chased the hares around the schoolyard until the end of the break, and then he changed them back into boys and girls.

The children didn't like being changed into animals, and when they got home and told their parents, the parents didn't like it, either, and they went to see a wise old woman to ask her advice. She told the parents what to tell the children they should do, and the parents told the children.

The following day, when the schoolmaster was about to change the boys and girls into hounds and hares, they asked him, "Master, can you change yourself into an animal?"

"Of course I can. What kind of animal do you want me to change into?"

"A pig."

So he tapped himself on the head with his magic wand and turned into a pig. But when he went to change himself back into the schoolmaster, he couldn't. He had forgotten that pigs don't have fingers, and so he couldn't pick up the wand to tap himself on the head.

He was so angry that the children had tricked him that he ran all over Ireland, tearing up the land with his tusks. So now where you see two ditches side by side, that is where he was running in a straight line with both tusks in the ground, and where you see only one ditch, that is where he was turning and had only one tusk in the ground.

He was running through Athlone, and as he was crossing the bridge over the Shannon, a woman hit him on the head with a big wooden hammer and killed him.

K1062. Dupe persuaded to transform self into animal. Cannot change back.

Bopolûchî
by Flora Annie Steel (1894)
Punjab, India

Once upon a time a number of young girls went to draw water at the village well, and while they were filling their jars, fell a-talking of their betrothals and weddings.

Said one, "My uncle will soon be coming with the bridal presents, and he is to bring the finest clothes imaginable."

Said a second, "And my uncle-in-law is coming, I know, bringing the most delicious sweetmeats you could think of."

Said a third, "Oh, my uncle will be here in no time, with the rarest jewels in the world."

But Bopolûchî, the prettiest girl of them all, looked sad, for she was an orphan, and had no one to arrange a marriage for her. Nevertheless she was too proud to remain silent, so she said gaily, "And my uncle is coming also, bringing me fine dresses, fine food, and fine jewels."

Now a wandering pedlar, who sold sweet scents and cosmetics of all sorts to the country women, happened to be sitting near the well, and heard what Bopolûchî said. Being much struck by her beauty and spirit, he determined to marry her himself, and the very next day, disguised as a well-to-do farmer, he came to Bopolûchî's house laden with trays upon trays full of fine dresses, fine food, and fine jewels; for he was not a real pedlar, but a wicked robber, ever so rich.

Bopolûchî could hardly believe her eyes, for everything was just as she had foretold, and the robber said he was her father's brother, who had been away in the world for years, and had now come back to arrange her marriage with one of his sons, her cousin.

Hearing this, Bopolûchî of course believed it all, and was ever so much pleased; so she packed up the few things she possessed in a bundle, and set off with the robber in high spirits.

But as they went along the road, a crow sitting on a branch croaked –

"Bopolûchî, 'tis a pity!
You have lost your wits, my pretty!
'Tis no uncle that relieves you,
But a robber who deceives you!"

"Uncle!" said Bopolûchî, "that crow croaks funnily. What does it say?"

"Pooh!" returned the robber, "all the crows in this country croak like that."

A little farther on they met a peacock, which, as soon as it caught sight of the pretty little maiden, began to scream –

> "Bopolûchî, 'tis a pity!
> You have lost your wits, my pretty!
> 'Tis no uncle that relieves you,
> But a robber who deceives you!"

"Uncle!" said the girl, "that peacock screams funnily. What does it say?"

"Pooh!" returned the robber, "all peacocks scream like that in this country."

By and by a jackal slunk across the road; the moment it saw poor pretty Bopolûchî it began to howl –

> "Bopolûchî, 'tis a pity!
> You have lost your wits, my pretty!
> 'Tis no uncle that relieves you,
> But a robber who deceives you!"

"Uncle!" said the maiden, "that jackal howls funnily. What does it say?"

"Pooh!" returned the robber, "all jackals howl like that in this country."

So poor pretty Bopolûchî journeyed on till they reached the robber's house. Then he told her who he was, and how he intended to marry her himself. She wept and cried bitterly, but the robber had no pity, and left her in charge of his old, oh! ever so old mother, while he went out to make arrangements for the marriage feast.

Now Bopolûchî had such beautiful hair that it reached right down to her ankles, but the old mother hadn't a hair on her old bald head.

"Daughter!" said the old, ever so old mother, as she was putting the bridal dress on Bopolûchî, "how did you manage to get such beautiful hair?"

"Well," replied Bopolûchî, "my mother made it grow by pounding my head in the big mortar for husking rice. At every stroke of the pestle my hair grew longer and longer. I assure you it is a plan that never fails."

"Perhaps it would make my hair grow!" said the old woman eagerly.

"Perhaps it would!" quoth cunning Bopolûchî.

So the old, ever so old mother put her head in the mortar, and Bopolûchî pounded away with such a will that the old lady died.

Then Bopolûchî dressed the dead body in the scarlet bridal dress, seated it on the low bridal chair, drew the veil well over the face, and put the spinning-wheel in front of it, so that when the robber came home he might think it was the bride. Then she put on the old mother's clothes, and seizing her own bundle, stepped out of the house as quickly as possible.

On her way home she met the robber, who was returning with a stolen millstone, to grind the corn for the wedding feast, on his head. She was dreadfully frightened, and slipped behind the hedge, so as not to be seen. But the robber, not recognising her in the old mother's dress, thought she was some strange woman from the neighbouring village, and so to avoid being seen he slipped behind the other hedge. Thus Bopolûchî reached home in safety.

Meanwhile, the robber, having come to his house, saw the figure in bridal scarlet sitting on the bridal chair spinning, and of course thought it was Bopolûchî,. So he called to her to help him down with the millstone, but she didn't answer. He called again, but still she didn't answer. Then he fell into a rage and threw the millstone at her head. The figure toppled over, and lo and behold! it was not Bopolûchî at all, but his old, ever so old mother! Whereupon the robber wept, and beat his breast, thinking he had killed her; but when he discovered pretty Bopolûchî had run away, he became wild with rage, and determined to bring her back somehow.

Now Bopolûchî was convinced that the robber would try to carry her off, so every night she begged a new lodging in some friend's house, leaving her own little bed in her own little house quite empty; but after a month or so she had come to the end of her friends, and did not like to ask any of them to give her shelter a second time. So she determined to brave it out and sleep at home, whatever happened; but she took a bill-hook to bed with her. Sure enough, in the very middle of the night four men crept in, and each seizing a leg of the bed, lifted it up and walked off, the robber himself having hold of the leg close behind her head. Bopolûchî was wide awake, but pretended to be fast asleep, until she came to a wild deserted spot, where the thieves were off their guard; then she whipped out the bill-hook, and in a twinkling cut off the heads of the two thieves at the foot of the bed. Turning round quickly, she did the same to the other thief at the head, but the robber himself ran away in a terrible fright, and scrambled like a wild cat up a tree close by before she could reach him.

"Come down!" cried brave Bopolûchî, brandishing the bill-hook, "and fight it out!"

But the robber would not come down, so Bopolûchî gathered all the sticks she could find, piled them round the tree, and set fire to them. Of course the tree caught fire also, and the robber, half stifled with the smoke, tried to jump down and was killed.

After that, Bopolûchî went to the robber's house and carried off all the gold and silver, jewels and clothes that were hidden there, coming back to the village so rich that she could marry anyone she

pleased. And that was the end of Bopolûchî's
adventures.

Source Author's Notes
"Bopolûchî" means Trickster.

Robber. The word used was *thag*, *lit.* a deceiver.
The *Thags* are a class but too well known in India as those
who make their living by deceiving and strangling
travellers. Meadows Taylor's somewhat sensational
book, *The Confessions of a Thug*, has made their doings
familiar enough, too, in England. In the Indian Penal Code
a *thag* is defined as a person habitually associated with
others for the purpose of committing robbery or child-
stealing by means of murder.

Crow's, etc., verses. The original words were –
Bopo Lûchî!
Aqlon ghuthî
Thag nâl thagî gaî.
Bopo Lûchî!
You have lost your wits,
And have been deceived by a *thag*.

Bridal scarlet. Every Panjâbî bride, however poor, wears a
dress of scarlet and gold for six months, and if rich, for
two years.

From *Tales of the Punjab* by Flora Annie Steel (1847-
1929), London & New York: Macmillan and Co., 1894.
Because this story is out of copyright and in the public
domain – belongs to everyone and no one – I have
reproduced it here verbatim.

O Ciprianillo: The Book of San Cipriano
Galicia, Spain
"The anonymous author ... was a great humorist."

This is a centuries-old money-spinning trick still current in Galicia and elsewhere.

There are many versions of The Book of San Cipriano (Saint Cyprian), known in Galicia as O Ciprianillo and elsewhere in Spain as El Ciprianillo, but two basic types. One is similar to the many grimoires – books of magic spells and rituals – that have been widely published for hundreds of years. That version is associated with contemporary Candomblé practices in Brazil and similar rites in other countries. The other is a detailed, though vague, cryptic and cabalistic, guide to the locations of hidden treasures, along with instructions on how to break the spells that conceal them and persuade the guardian spirits or demons to give them up. Most Ciprianillos are a combination of both types, as is my copy, an 80-page Galician-language paperback published in Vigo in 1974: *Os Tesouros [The Treasures] de Galicia: O Ciprianillo*; translation, notes and introduction by Xosé María Álvarez Blázquez.

The key section of the book, "Accounts of the Treasures and Spells", lists 174 locations in Galicia where buried treasure supposedly can be found. Example: "In the middle of the castle of Pazos, at a great depth, there is a gold mine guarded by a live calf. If you want to get the gold, don't touch the calf." Another: "In the water channel of San Xohán de Amerín, above the banks of black stone, there is a two-wheeled cart with brass sides full of gold coins. In this hiding place there is an enchanted man with a cattle prod. He won't kill you if you want to take the treasure. Tell him: 'By the power of the *mouro* gold, I request that you go and join the *mouros*, your relatives, and leave me content.'"

A *mouro* is a sort of fairy or earth spirit or elemental who guards gold and other treasures. Mouros are often conflated with the Muslim hordes collectively called

Moors (*mouros* in Galician, *moros* in Spanish) who conquered Spain in the eighth century. They buried their valuables when they went into battle, assuming that they would return one day to recover them. Many didn't.

A standard account of Cipriano's life tells us that he was born in the third century in Antioch of rich and powerful parents. He wrote many books of magic spells and commanded infernal spirits. At the age of thirty, he was asked by a young man to help persuade a Christian woman named Justina to marry him. Cipriano called on his demonic servants, but their efforts were ineffective, because Justina was protected by the Virgin, Christ and the Cross of San Bartolomé that appeared in the palm of her right hand. Infuriated and embarrassed, Cipriano confronted Lucifer, who explained, "The Christian God is lord of all creation, and I am subject to His orders. I am powerless to act against anyone who uses the sign of the cross."

"Well, if that's the case," said Cipriano, "I hereby renounce you, and I will become a disciple of Christ."

Unreliable history sources and legend say that Cipriano became bishop of Antioch, and Justina head of a convent. They were martyred together on 26 September 304. Reliable history says that there was never a bishop of Antioch named Cipriano, and the Catholic Church has removed him from the list of officially acknowledged saints.

According to one version of the Ciprianillo, Cipriano stopped two young men who were fighting to the death over the woman they both loved, Celia. Cipriano asked Celia which of them she preferred. She said she loved neither. Cipriano instantly fell in love with her, but she told him he also had no chance, as she intended to be a nun. A stranger came to Cipriano's house asking for hospitality, saw he was sad, and offered to help. It was Lucifer, the Ultimate Trickster. He showed Cipriano several visions, in two of which Celia professed her love for him, and then Lucifer gave him the same powers on

110

condition that he study a book of spells for a year and agree to give him his body and soul.

This book, written in Hebrew, was later passed on by Lucifer to the monk Jonas Sufurino. He explained that the pages were bathed in the lagoon of the Red Dragons and suffused with spells that made them indestructible. Also, if the book was lost, or even if Jonas threw it away, it would return to him because, "This book carries between its pages the cabalistic signs of the Red Dragon and the Infernal Goat." With no previous knowledge of Hebrew, Jonas was able to read the book perfectly. There were two notes on the title page:

> We dedicate this book to the new adept in the hidden sciences. – Lucifer

> I declare that this book has shown me the true wisdom through which I have gained absolute power over all creation. – Cipriano the Wizard

As Jonas turned the pages, the Dragon and the Goat came to life and stepped out of the book and promised to serve him. He translated the book into German in AD 1001, averring in the Introduction: "I, Jonas Sufurino, a monk of the monastery of Brooken ... declare to the whole world that what this book contains is the truth." Included are potions to stop loving someone unworthy of you; potions to obtain the favours of a woman; a spell to make someone marry you ("Take a piece of magnetic stone and go to the church when they are saying Mass or when there are two candles burning ..."); a prayer to win the lottery; a recipe for a powder to make a woman dance naked ("Throw it into the air in the direction of the woman, and it will take immediate effect").

The first documented mention of a book with the title "Book of San Cipriano" is in an Inquisition trial of 1802 in Galicia. Modern consensus is that the Ciprianillo was written in French by a Frenchified Galician and published in Paris as early as the 16th century, but more likely the end of the 18th century. That the unnamed author was Galician is strongly suggested by the fact that he was intimately familiar with Galician magical beliefs and the ancient sites and topography of Galicia.

There are several versions of the book currently in print. I first encountered the 1974 edition – the first Galician language one – in the reference section of the Ourense Municipal Library about the year 2000. The next time I looked for it, it was missing – for a good reason: it went out of print, and someone desperately needed it to seek his fortune. It purports to be a copy of an 11th-century document currently held in a library in Barcelona, the Biblioteca Académica Peninsular Catalaní, "where it can be seen by the curious who ask for it." (Don't bother asking; it's not there.) The original is said to be kept chained, apparently because it's dangerous, in either the library of the Cathedral in Santiago de Compostela or the library of the University of Compostela. (It's not in either place.) The first sentence in Álvarez Blázquez' introduction is: "The anonymous author of the book popularly known as *O Ciprianillo* was a great humorist."

The first chapter is "A True Story that Occurred in the Kingdom of Galicia", in which a poor farmer living near Paris sells his soul to the Devil in exchange for riches. The Devil directs him to Galicia: "In that distant land you will find more buried gold than in all the other provinces [of Spain] ... more than a hundred enchanted treasures ... the riches of more than six kingdoms." Then he mentions twenty localities around the city of Ourense, whose name derives from the Galician word for "gold" (*ouro*) and which was built on the site of the Roman city of Auria, *aurum* being Latin for "gold".

The sceptical reader will dismiss the above accounts of the Book of San Cipriano as flim-flam and cynically wish the treasure seekers well in their fruitless search for hidden riches and hope the fresh air and exercise will clear their minds of nonsense.

However, besides the probability that some unretrieved Moorish treasures lie concealed somewhere, there is another explanation for the gold fever. Galicia was the home of the most important gold mine in the Roman Empire. Over the course of 250 years, beginning in the first century AD, the Romans extracted 1,650,000kg (3,637,627lb) of gold by an intricate hydraulic method – a sort of liquid strip mining – in Las Médulas on the Galicia-León border, leaving a desolate "cultural landscape" bizarrely designated a World Heritage Site in 1997.

So the combination of gold possibly overlooked by Roman miners and wealth possibly left unclaimed by defeated Moors lends credibility to the idea of treasures concealed under magic spells by the mouros. It remains a powerful incentive to buy or steal a collection of instructions on how to find them and break the enchantments and deal with guardian spirits. Archaeologists have reported local stories of people who believe that the petroglyphs (rock carvings) at ancient sites in Galicia indicate the presence of gold and show exactly where it is concealed. They arrive, Ciprianillo in hand, to dig and even dynamite the sites. It doesn't seem to occur to the seekers that a person who knows where 174 treasures are buried would be more likely to retrieve them himself than announce the locations to the world. The entrepreneur who writes such a book and sells it to the gullible is the only one guaranteed to make a fortune. Las Médulas may be played out, but *los crédulos* have been mined profitably for centuries.

Buenaventura Aparicio Casado concludes her comprehensive study of oral tradition associated with 525 archaeological sites in Galicia, *Mouras, Serpientes, Tesoros y Otros Encantos*, with this wistful comment: "The times are not propitious for magical thinking and fantasy, and, sooner rather than later, this folklore of *mouros* will be only a memory preserved in the material we have collected."

But meanwhile, the tradition remains alive and vibrant. Pena Molexa, near Ferrol in northwest Galicia, is said to have the most legends in the world. Local people gather

113

for an all-night party on the mountain, believed to be an ancient Celtic ceremonial site, every Summer Solstice – Saint John's Night – to celebrate the stories attached to the place. (The ritual is well represented on the internet.) One tells of a moura who is enchanted in the form of a rock and appears in the flesh only at the Solstice, surrounded by gold and jewels. If a man sees her and selects one of the jewels instead of her, the moura bursts into tears and becomes rock again, and the jewel turns to coal. If a man chooses her over the jewel, the enchantment will be broken, but that has never happened. Another legend says that a man took a copy of the Ciprianillo to the top of the mountain and read it from front to back, then, word by word, from back to front. That broke the charm, and he saw three mules laden with gold coming toward him. He took all the gold home and never returned to Pena Molexa, knowing that greed would result in misfortune.

The following three accounts show how deeply embedded in Galician culture is the notion of hidden gold. The first two incidents were related to me by the great-uncle of a friend in the village of A Pobra de Trives, in the middle of gold country near Ourense.

A group of men arrived at his farm one day, asking for his permission to search on his land for a hoard they believed might be there. They had a copy of the Ciprianillo with them, apparently the 1974 edition listing the 174 locations. He gave them permission and never heard what the results were.

My friend's great-uncle had been a member of a local semi-professional band so popular in the region that a sculpture of them occupies a prominent spot on the main street of Trives. A fellow band member was known to be searching for treasure with the aid of the Ciprianillo. One day he abruptly quit his day job and left town, never to be seen again. It was rumoured that he had struck gold.

A teacher at a language school in Ourense, where I have visited a few times to tell Irish stories in English, told me that one of her students told her this story. In the nearby village where she lived, the people held the wide-

114

spread belief that where a vein of tar is found in the ground there is a vein of gold not far away. They had discovered a vein of tar and were going to hire a mechanical digger to search for the vein of gold. The teacher hadn't heard if they had been successful, and on a subsequent visit to the school I was disappointed to find that the teacher had left, and no one could tell me the end of the story. But I understand why the Ourense audiences take my Irish tale of the leprechaun and his pot of gold so seriously.

Daniel O'Connell
Ireland

Daniel O'Connell (1775-1847), the Great Liberator, campaigned for equal rights for Catholics and was the most widely popular politician in Ireland in his day. The extent of the people's love for him is demonstrated by the many migratory international folk tales they have attached to him.

A man fell out of a boat while fishing, went under the water, surfaced, couldn't swim and was drowning. Another man in the boat pulled him out with a hook and saved his life, but the hook caught in the drowning man's eye and put it out. Afterwards, the saved man sued the rescuer for his injury. Daniel O'Connell – "a young lad" or specifically seven years old at the time – and other boys heard about the case and were discussing it.

"The solution to that dispute is simple," Dan said. "Throw the man overboard in the same place, and let no one try to help him. If he saves himself, his rescuer is guilty of injuring him. If he drowns, the rescuer is not guilty."

(Variant: adult Dan as a lawyer overheard boys in the street discussing the case; one boy gave that judgement, and Dan appropriated it.)

115

Word of Daniel's judgement came to the ears of the legal experts, and they applied it to the case. When the plaintiff heard it, he withdrew his complaint.

Many versions of this story have been collected in Ireland, but it's a variant of an international folk tale dating at least as far back as the 13th century.

J1172. Judgment as rebuke to unjust plaintiff.

J1172.3. Ungrateful animal returned to captivity. (See "The Farmer and the Wolf and the Three Judges" chapter.)

J123. Wisdom of child decides lawsuit.

One of O'Connell's most widely quoted remarks is: "Sins against morals are not as bad as sins against faith." His devoted biographer, Thomas Clarke Luby, admitted: "He is said to have not infrequently forgotten his marriage vows." O'Connell was reputed to have left countless illegitimate offspring up and down the country. It was said that if you threw a stone over the wall of an orphanage it would hit one of his children. He was walking along a road one day, and a young boy asked him for money. Dan gave him some and told him he'd give him more the next time he saw him. The lad took a shortcut and appeared on the road again in front of Dan and asked him for the promised money. Dan recognized him as one of his children because of his cleverness.

O'Connell was acting for the defence in a case in which a hat allegedly belonging to the defendant was found at the scene of the crime by a policeman, who was a prosecution witness. O'Connell peered inside the hat. There was no name on the sweatband, but he pretended to spell out:

"J.A.M.E.S.F.O.G.A.R.T.Y. Is that the name you found inside this hat?" he asked the policeman.

"It is."

"Did you see that name inside the hat?"

"I did."

"And is this the same hat you found at the scene of the crime?"

116

"It is."

Dan showed the judge that there was no name written in the hat, thereby discrediting the policeman as a witness. Case dismissed.

He was defending a man in court and advised him to pretend to be mentally incompetent by answering every question with, "Have a bulls-eye." (A bulls-eye is a popular ball-shaped boiled sweet with black and white stripes.) The judge found him unfit for trial and dismissed the case. When Dan asked the client for his fee, the client said, "Have a bulls-eye."

The same story is the basis of a 15th-century French play, *The Farce of Master Pathelin*.

K1655. The lawyer's mad client. On the advice of a lawyer, the client feigns insanity when arraigned in court. When the fee is demanded, he still feigns insanity.

O'Connell was at dinner in England carving a roast pig. An Englishman said, "Whatever you do to that animal I'll do the same to you." Dan "stuck his finger up under its tail, and brought down some of the stuffing and ate it. He then took down his breeches and says to the man, 'Will you do that to me?'"

(From the National Folklore Collection 871:10-11; collected 1934-40 by Máire Ní Sheasnáin from Mrs Margaret Fleming, Ballalley, Carrick on Suir, Co. Tipperary.)

The same story is told about Carreño, a famous wit in 19th-century Málaga, carving a turkey.

O'Connell was walking down a road in a part of Ireland that he was not familiar with. He saw a barefoot man resting against a tree at the side of the road and asked him the way to a certain town. The man simply jerked a big toe to indicate the direction.

"I've never seen anyone as lazy as you," Dan said. "I'll give you a shilling if you can show me something lazier."

Without moving his head, the man glanced down at his shirt pocket. Amused, Dan put a shilling in the pocket.

A similar story is told about Jonathan Swift and his servant "Jack".

W111.5.3. Lazy man asked direction only points with his foot.

Curran and the Innkeeper
Ireland

As a student at Trinity College in Dublin, John Philpot Curran (1750-1817) was nicknamed "Stuttering Jack" for his disastrous attempt at a maiden speech before the debating society, when he became completely tongue-tied. He was eventually acclaimed as "the most popular advocate of his time" and a devastatingly effective orator. Daniel O'Connell dubbed him "the Irish Cicero". He is the source of the political adage "Eternal vigilance is the price of liberty," which he coined in an 1808 speech in Dublin. He used his sharp wit to puncture pomposity and defend the underdog. Many migratory international folk tales have become attached to him, of which this is probably the most famous.

A wealthy merchant was attending a fair. Worried that his pocket might be picked in the crowds, he lodged £100 with the innkeeper, neglecting to obtain a receipt and without witnesses. After the fair, he asked the innkeeper to return his money.

"What £100?"

With no receipt and no witnesses, the merchant was stymied. He went to Curran for advice. Curran told him to go to the innkeeper with witnesses and say that he must have been mistaken and probably left the £100 elsewhere, and then to lodge another £100 with him in front of the witnesses. Then he was to go back to the innkeeper without witnesses and ask for his money back. He got it.

The next step, Curran said, was to return to the innkeeper again, this time with the witnesses, and ask for his £100. The innkeeper now realized that he had been counter-tricked and gave him the (original) £100.

King Matthias the Just
Hungary

According to the *Hungarian World Encyclopedia*, the 32-year reign of Matthias (1443-1490) "represented the pinnacle of Hungary's greatness. ... He was the most popular king in Hungary." Educated in the humanities, he established an impressive library and founded print shops and bookshops and encouraged scholarship. Intellectuals, artists, professors and students flocked to Hungary as a centre of culture and learning.

Perhaps inspired by legends of kings travelling incognito through their kingdoms to monitor the well-being of their subjects, and certainly because of a genuine desire to ensure justice for all, Matthias would disguise himself and a companion as students and mingle with the common people. The 16th-century historian Gaspar Heltai reports this story as a legend.

Matthias was travelling through the country with a retinue, and when they arrived at the village of Gilau he left his followers at the castle and went alone disguised as a student to the nearby city of Cluj, where he had been born, to investigate the social conditions. He watched as poor people were forced to carry firewood for the judge, with no benefit to the general public, and he objected. He was whipped and forced to join the commoners and work for free. He managed to write on three pieces of timber in the judge's yard: "King Matthias was here. Where is justice?" He was released at the end of the day and returned to Gilau.

The following day, he arrived in Cluj as himself at the head of his retinue in full regalia and asked how the laws protecting the poor people were being observed. He was told that the city was fully compliant. He then located the

pieces of wood he had written on to expose the hypocrisy
of the judge and had him severely punished.

Digging for Treasure
Punjab, India

There was a barber who was so incompetent that he
always drew blood whenever he shaved a person or cut his
hair. When he sliced off a man's ear, he lost the few
customers that were left. His wife was furious.

"You're too stupid to make a living, and I don't want
to starve. Go to the king and ask him to give you
something so we can eat."

So the barber went to the king and said, "My wife sent
me to ask you to give me something."

"What sort of something?" said the king.

"She didn't say."

The king saw that the man was not very bright.

"Where do you live?"

The barber told him.

"I own a field in that area. I'll give it to you."

The king drew a map to show the barber where the
field was, and the barber took it home to show his wife.

"Did the king give you something?"

He showed her the map.

"A field? We can't eat a field, and we don't have
money to buy a plough and horses to till the soil and seeds
to sow, and we'll starve before the crop grows anyway.
But let's see this something the king gave you."

They went to the field and discovered why the king
was so willing to give it away. It was waste ground full of
stones: not a few big rocks that might be pushed out of the
way, but stones large enough to break a plough or cripple
a horse, and much too many to clear by hand.

"This field is worse than useless," the wife said. "We'd
have to dig it up by hand, and that would take far too
long."

But then she got an idea. She told her husband to follow her and do exactly what she did. They walked slowly around the field, parting the weeds and peering closely at the ground. Eventually a thief walking along the road stopped and asked what they were looking for.

"I'll tell you if you promise you won't tell anyone else," said the woman.

"I promise."

"This field belonged to my grandfather. Just before he died he told me that he had buried five pots of gold in this field, but he didn't say where, and we're looking for them."

The thief gathered six other thieves and told them about the gold. That night they went to the field and dug here and there until it looked as if it had been ploughed and harrowed. Of course, they found nothing.

In the morning, the barber's wife went to the field and was delighted to see that her plan had worked and the field was ready for planting. She got seeds on credit with the promise that she would return them threefold after the harvest, and when she explained the situation to the man at the grocery store, he gave her credit for food. The crop was successful, and she was able to pay bills, with enough gold coins left over to fill a crock.

The thieves noticed the bountiful harvest and demanded a share of the profits.

"We did all the hard work. You tricked us into tilling the field."

"I told you there was gold in the ground. I found it and you didn't."

The thieves suspected that there was gold in the house as well, and one of them hid in the house so he could look for it during the night. The woman noticed him but didn't let on. She hatched a plan to discourage them.

"Did you put the gold in a safe place?" the barber asked her.

"Yes. It's in a crock with sweetmeats on top in the niche by the front door."

The thief heard this, and when the couple had gone to bed, he grabbed the crock and ran out to share his booty with his companions, not knowing that the woman had filled the crock with rotten food and other household waste of the most unappetizing sort. They opened it and confidently stuffed handfuls of the supposed sweetmeats into their mouths before they realized that the woman had played another trick on them. They vowed revenge.

Another of the band of thieves hid in the house the next night, but once again the woman noticed him. When the barber asked what she had done with the gold, she answered, "I moved it out of the house for safety. It's in a gourd hanging in the tree."

It was, in fact, a hornets' nest, and the thieves' encounter with it laid them up in hospital for a month. Just when she thought they had given up, one night she heard whispering outside an open window. She got her husband's razor and waited. When a nose appeared in the window, she sliced off the tip of it. The thief thought he had cut his nose on something, and the others tried to creep through the window until all except their cautious chief had lost the tips of their noses. They decided to retreat and try again when they had healed. The barber's wife gathered up the nose tips and put them in a bag.

A short time later, the weather was too warm to sleep indoors, so the barber and his wife moved their beds outside, thinking the thieves had learned their lesson. However, back came the thieves, this time bent on revenge. To their pleasant surprise, they found the couple asleep under the stars. They carefully picked up the woman's bed and carried it away on their shoulders. The movement woke her up, but she pretended to be asleep while she desperately searched for a way to escape.

They stopped under a banyan tree, and she managed to grab on to a branch and swing into the tree just as the thieves put the bed down to have a rest. Six of them had not fully recovered from the shortening of their noses, so the chief stood watch while they slept. This gave the barber's wife an idea. She raised her nightgown so the top of it covered her head and began to sing softly. The head thief looked up and, since he had an exaggerated opinion of his attractiveness to women, assumed she was a fairy woman flirting with him.

"Come down here to me, my lovely. Don't be afraid."

But she continued singing, so he climbed up to her. When he came close, she turned away.

"What's the matter? Don't you like me?"

"I don't trust men with long noses. They're always fickle."

He now regretted that his nose hadn't been shortened along with those of his companions.

"But I'm the most faithful man in the world."

"I'll only believe that if I taste your tongue to see if there are any lies on it. Stick your tongue out."

He did, and she bit off the tip.

"Ya!" he screamed, and he tumbled out of the tree and fell sprawling and squalling on the ground.

The noise woke up his companions.

"What happened?" they said.

"Ee ih eye ung aw," he explained, holding his tongue to stop the bleeding.

"He's gone mad," said one of the thieves. "He's speaking in tongues."

"Ung, ung."

"He's bewitched," said another thief.

"Ee ih eye ung aw," he repeated, pointing to the strange figure in the tree.

The barber's wife flapped her arms and howled. The thieves took to their heels and ran without a backward look. The woman climbed down from the tree and carried her bed on her head back to her house.

The thieves finally concluded that it was useless trying to steal the gold, so they went to the king and complained about how they had worked so hard to till the couple's field but got no share of the profits. The king asked the barber's wife for her side of the argument, and when he heard the full story he threw the thieves in prison and hired the woman as his advisor.

Abridged and rewritten from "The Barber's Clever Wife" in *Tales of the Punjab* by Flora Annie Steel (1847-1929), Macmillan, 1894.

H588.7. Father's counsel: find treasure within a foot of the ground. (Sons dig everywhere and thus loosen soil of vineyard, which becomes fruitful.)

K685. Escape by catching hold of limbs of tree while passing under it.

The Doctor and Death
Spain, Basque Country, Ireland

Once upon a time there was a man who lived happily ever after, but that's just the beginning of the story.

All his life, a poor shoemaker had nothing to eat but beans, cornbread and cheese. The people in his village were so poor they only wore their shoes on Sundays, because they couldn't afford to buy new shoes. The only work the shoemaker had was to repair their shoes, which meant that he was in fact only a shoe repairman, and you don't make much money repairing shoes, especially shoes that people only wear on Sundays.

The shoemaker made just enough money to buy enough food so that he didn't starve to death, but he could never afford to buy enough to have a really satisfying meal. He had never in his life known the feeling of a full belly.

One day he said to himself, "This is no way to live. I'd rather die than go on like this." So he sold all his shoemaking tools and bought himself food for a real meal – a big piece of dried cod, a fat, tasty chicken, potatoes, vegetables, and a bottle of the best Rioja wine. This was going to be his last meal, and when he sat down, he said to himself, "No one has ever given me anything in my life, and I'm not going to share this meal with anyone."

Saint Peter was listening, and he said to himself, "We'll see about this."

Saint Peter went to Jesus Christ and told Him what the shoemaker said, and Jesus Christ said to Saint Peter, "Go down to earth disguised as a beggar, and ask him to give you some of his food. Surely he won't refuse to give alms to a beggar."

Saint Peter went to the shoemaker's house and knocked on the door, just as the shoemaker was about to put the first forkful in his mouth. The shoemaker opened the door, and Saint Peter said, "I'm hungry. Will you share your meal with me?"

The shoemaker replied, "No. No one has ever given me anything in my life, and I'm not going to share this meal with anyone."

Saint Peter said, "Do you know who I am?"

The shoemaker said, "No."

"I'm Saint Peter," said Saint Peter.

"I don't care if you're Jesus Christ. Go away."

So Saint Peter went back up to Heaven and told Jesus Christ what had happened. Jesus Christ said, "I'll send someone else, and then we'll see what he does."

And He sent Death, disguised as a beggar.

Death went to the shoemaker's house and knocked on the door. The shoemaker opened the door, and Death said, "Will you share some of your meal with me?"

The shoemaker replied, "No. No one has ever given me anything in my life, and I'm not going to share this meal with anyone."

Death said, "Do you know who I am?"

The shoemaker said, "I don't care if you're Saint Peter or Jesus Christ Himself. Go away."

"I'm Death," said Death.

"Death, my old friend," said the shoemaker. "I'm happy to see you. I've been expecting you, though not quite so soon. Come in and sit down and have something to eat."

And the shoemaker shared what he thought was his last meal with Death. At the end of the meal, Death said, "You've been very kind to share your meal with me, and I want to give you a reward. What would you like?"

The shoemaker said, "I don't want anything. This was my last meal, and now that I've known the feeling of a full belly, I'm ready to go with you."

But Death said, "No, no, it's not your time yet. I want to give you something. I'll make you a doctor."

The shoemaker said, "But I don't know anything about diseases, and I don't know how to write prescriptions."

"Don't worry," said Death. "You can make up any cure you wish. When you visit a patient, you will see me, although no one else will be able to see me. If I'm sitting next to the head of the patient, that patient is mine, and nothing you or any doctor can do will save them. You can say that the person will die, and when they die you will be seen as an expert. But if you see me sitting next to the feet of the patient, they'll recover no matter what you give them, and you'll get the credit. You'll become a rich and famous doctor, and you will always have enough to eat."

The shoemaker liked the sound of that, and he agreed.

"The Queen is very ill," said Death. "The King has called all the wisest doctors in the kingdom, but none of them can do anything to cure her. They're only waiting for her to die. But it's not her time yet. Make a soup of the leftover chicken we had for dinner and take it to the Queen. Tell the King she'll recover if she eats the soup. When she recovers, that will be the making of your reputation."

So the shoemaker dressed in his best clothes, which because he was a poor man were not very good at all, and went to the palace. He told the palace guards that he had come to cure the Queen, but they laughed at him and told him to go away. He shouted loudly, "I've come to cure the Queen," and the King heard him. He was desperate, so he ordered the shoemaker to be brought into the palace.

When the shoemaker went into the Queen's room, he saw Death sitting at her feet. He gave the Queen a spoonful of the chicken soup, and he told the King that the Queen would begin to recover immediately. All the doctors laughed, but the following day the Queen was

126

sitting up in her bed eating the soup by herself, and the day after that she was out of bed and walking around.

The King was so grateful that he gave the shoemaker a bag of gold and a fine suit of clothes, and a coach and horses and a coach driver to go with them. But the wise doctors who had failed to cure the Queen were envious. They worked out a plan to expose the shoemaker as a fake.

One of the doctors pretended to be seriously ill, and they called the shoemaker to come and cure him. When the shoemaker arrived, he saw Death sitting next to the doctor's head, and he said he could do nothing, and that the doctor was going to die that night. The other doctors laughed, because they knew – or thought they knew – that the doctor was perfectly healthy and was not going to die. But he died that night.

That was the beginning of the shoemaker's career as a doctor. Word spread throughout the kingdom, and people came from all over to be cured by the doctor or be told that they would not recover. Everyone that the doctor said would die, died, and everyone that he said would recover, recovered.

One day, he was called to see a young girl. Death was sitting next to her head. But the girl was so young, and her parents were so sad but so full of hope because they thought the doctor could cure her, that he picked her up and turned her around in the bed, so that Death was now sitting at her feet.

The girl recovered, but the following morning the doctor woke up to see Death sitting next to *his* head.

"You played a nice trick on me yesterday," said Death, "and since you cheated me of a victim, you will have to take her place."

"You're right," said the doctor, "but will you wait until I finish saying a prayer before you take me?"

Death agreed to wait until the doctor finished saying a prayer, and the doctor said, "Hail Mary, full of grace ..." And he said no more. He didn't finish saying the prayer, and so Death was not able to take him. Death went away, very angry at being tricked again.

A few weeks later, the doctor was riding in his coach, when he saw a man hanging from a tree. He told his driver to stop and said, "What's happened there?"

"Ah, it seems that some poor man has committed suicide."

"Well," said the doctor, "we have to say a prayer for his unfortunate soul. Hail Mary, full of grace ..." And this time the doctor said the complete prayer. When he finished, the hanged man reached up and loosened the rope around his neck and climbed down from the tree. He came over to the doctor's coach. It was Death.

"Now that you've finished your prayer," said Death, "it's time for you to come with me."

"You're right," said the doctor. "I'll go with you. But I've made a lot of money and I have a lot of property to dispose of to my family and friends. I have to write a will to say what goes to whom."

The doctor took a short candle and lit it.

"Will you wait just until this candle burns to the end before you take me?"

"I'll wait that long," said Death. "But when that candle has burned to the end, you will come with me."

As soon as Death said that, the doctor blew out the flame. He keeps that candle locked away in a safe place, and as far as I know, the doctor is still living happily ever after, and that is why this story has no end.

K557. Death cheated by moving bed.

K551.9. Let me live as long as this candle lasts.

The Fairy Fort Is on Fire
Ireland

The Irish name of Slievenamon in County Tipperary is Sliabh na mBan Finn – the Hill of Fionn's Women. It got its name from the time Fionn mac Cumhaill organized a race to the top of the hill for all the women who fancied him. The prize to the winner was Fionn himself.

An ancient monument, whether a 12th-century Anglo-Norman defensive motte or a circular earthen bank known as a rath or a lis, or a 5000-year-old cairn or passage tomb, is often called the "fairy fort" locally. A cairn believed to be a passage tomb lies near the peak of the 2363-foot (720m) Slievenamon.

There was a woman living at the foot of Slievenamon who loved spinning and all the processes that go into preparing the raw wool: washing, drying, teasing, and carding or combing. But housework bored her. She was spinning late one Saturday night, while her husband and children were all asleep. In fact, it was after midnight, which meant that she was working on a Sunday. It also happened to be Samhain Eve (Halloween), one of the nights when the gateways between this world and the Otherworld are open.

She had neglected to smoor the fire – smother it in ashes so the *gríosach* (embers) would be preserved overnight to seed the fire in the morning. As usual, she hadn't thrown out the water that had been used to wash the children's feet or done the washing up from the evening meal. The broom handle was carelessly left in the cold grey ashes on the hearth.

She had just got up from the spinning wheel – with the iron band still on it – to get ready for bed, when she heard a voice outside:

"Gríosach, where are you?"

The gríosach answered, "I'm in the grate blazing away."

Another voice called out, "Feet water, where you are?"

"I'm in the tub."

Another, "Dishes, where are you?"

"In the sink, waiting to be washed."

Another, "Broom, where are you?"

"Lying down with my handle in the ashes."

Another, "Spinning wheel band, where are you?"

"Still on the wheel."

A chorus of voices: "Gríosach, feet water, dishes, broom, spinning wheel band, open the door and let us in."

All those things rushed to the door and opened it. Twelve fierce horned women stormed in. Their faces looked old as time and ugly as mortal sin. One had a horn on her head, another had two horns, another had three, and so on to the one with twelve horns.

"Woman," said one of them, "put more turf on the fire and boil water for our tea."

"There's no water in the house," she said.

"Take that sieve and fetch water from the well."

"In a sieve?"

"Do what you're told or you'll regret it."

The woman took the sieve, relieved to get out of the house, and went to the well. Of course, when she put water in the sieve it poured right through, and she burst into tears, afraid of what would happen if she didn't make tea for the terrible women.

"Mix moss and clay to plaster the sieve," came a voice from the well.

It sounded like her long-dead grandmother, but the woman never paused nor pondered till she had the plastered sieve filled with water.

"Now, my pet," the voice from the well said, and by that the woman knew it was her grandmother, "go back to the house and run in and say, 'The fairy fort is on fire.' Those women will run out to save their children, but they will return very angry when they find they have been tricked. While they're gone, smoor the fire, throw out the feet water, wash the dishes, fasten the broom across the door, and take the band off the spinning wheel."

The woman went back to the house, ran in and shouted, "The fairy fort is on fire." The women fell over one another rushing out the door, crying, "My children, my children."

She did all the things her grandmother's voice told her to do, and, just as she had finished, the horned women returned and called out:

"Gríosach, let us in."

130

The gríosach answered, "I can't move. I'm smoored."
"Feet water, let us in."
"I can't. I'm out here under your feet."
"Dishes, let us in."
"We can't. We're washed and drying in the rack."
"Broom, let us in."
"I can't. I'm barring the door."
"Spinning wheel band, let us in."
"I can't. I'm off the wheel."

The fairy women left, cursing the woman and her house and everything in it but in vain, because ever after that night the woman took care to put the house in order before going to bed, especially on Samhain Eve and Bealtaine Eve. And she never worked again on a Sunday.

G272.7.1. Beam across door protects from witch.

The Father of Farts
Syria

A wealthy and avaricious judge lived in the city of Tarabulus in Syria in the eighth century, during the time of Harun al-Rashid "the Just", the capricious and despotic ruler of the Middle East who became caliph after the mysterious death of his older brother.

The judge was widely respected for his position and feared because of the severity of his decisions. His greed was matched by his miserliness. He kept only one servant, an old woman. If a neighbour or colleague dropped in, the judge would call ostentatiously to the servant, "Lay the gold-fringed cloth!" The cloth would be spread on the table, and the visitor naturally expected to be fed, but no food would appear. When the visitor left, the old woman would serve the usual meal for the judge and herself consisting of stale bread and onions.

One day, a man who wished to influence the judge regarding an upcoming court case said to him, "It isn't right for you to live alone with only a servant. Why don't you take a wife? I have a beautiful daughter who would suit you."

The judge accepted the offer, and he and the girl were married in his house. After the ceremony, the guests waited patiently for the expected feast to be served, and as time went on and no food appeared, they peeked into the kitchen and saw that no fire was lighted, so they drifted away hungry. The young bride was polite and well brought up, and when the order of "Lay the gold-fringed cloth" was followed by three pieces of stale bread and three onions, she tried to conceal her disappointment. The judge and the servant eagerly devoured their food, but the girl was unable to swallow even a bite. She went to bed hungry and bitter.

After three days of this, she sent a message to her father asking him to take her home. When the servant told the judge what his new wife had done, he cursed the girl, greatly dishonoured her by cutting off her hair, recited the formal ritual "I divorce you, I divorce you, I divorce you," and threw her into the street and slammed the door.

Another man, seeking favour with the judge, offered his daughter, with the same result. And the next, and the next, until the mothers of the city pronounced the judge unfit for marriage.

One evening as the judge was walking along a road, he spied a woman riding toward him on a mule. As she drew closer, he saw that she was fair of form and face with an air of quality and intelligence.

"Where do you come from, my lady?" he asked with a bow.

"Along this road," she replied.

"I can see that, but from what city?"

"Mosul."

(Mosul was the prosperous capital of neighbouring Mesopotamia at this time.)

"Are you married?"

"No."

"Then if you would like to be my wife, I'd like to be your husband."

"Tell me where you live, and I'll give you my answer tomorrow," she replied with a flirtatious, promising glance.

She already knew what her answer would be. She knew who he was and where he lived, and she had come to Tarabulus to marry him for a reason that will become clear.

In the morning, she sent him a message saying she would be pleased to become his wife if he provided a dowry of fifty dinars. His innate selfishness gave him a battle, but he sent fifty dinars with his servant, who brought the bride to his house. There was the usual wedding ceremony and non-banquet, after which the guests went away empty-stomached as usual. Then the judge commanded, "Lay the gold-fringed cloth!" The cloth was laid, and the usual stale bread and onions were served. The new bride ate with gusto and said, "I thank Allah for an excellent meal."

The judge responded: "I thank Allah for sending me a perfect wife who understands the little and the large of life."

The following morning, while the judge was away at a council meeting, the woman made an inspection of the house. She came to a cabinet that was secured by three locks and three iron bars. She found a small hole and looked inside, and was not surprised to see copper jars heaped with gold and silver coins. She took the stalk of a long palm branch and put a sticky paste on one end, and she manoeuvred it through the hole and picked up some of the gold pieces.

She gave the coins to the servant and said, "Go out and buy rolls and rice and lamb and fruits and pastries."

The servant was astonished, and when she returned and the woman shared the tasty meal with her, she said, "I have never eaten such fine food."

"We will eat like this every day if you keep it a secret from the judge."

The servant agreed of course.

133

When the judge returned for his dinner and called out, "Lay the gold-fringed cloth!" he was served with the plentiful leftovers. He ate greedily, and when he was full he said, "Where did you get this wonderful food?"

"I have relatives in this city," his wife told him, "and one of them was generous enough to share these modest provisions with me."

The judge thanked Allah for providing such a resourceful and well-connected wife.

On the following day, her probe with the palm branch was again fruitful, and she sent the servant out to buy a lamb stuffed with pistachios and other rich dishes. This time, she invited the neighbour women, who were extremely grateful for the treat.

"We'll have more of these meetings," she told them, "as long as we keep it a secret from the judge."

When the judge came home for his dinner, he was amazed at the even more luxurious meal that his wife had prepared, and asked her where it had come from.

"My aunt, who lives in this city, sent me these little leftovers," she said.

And so it continued for a year. By then, the judge had feasted so sumptuously that his girth had grown well beyond substantial, and the people coined a saying to describe something enormous: "as big as the judge's belly". It was now time for the wife to put the finishing touches on the scheme that had brought her to Tarabulus: revenge for the unfortunate young women the judge had rejected and humiliated.

It fitted her plan perfectly that a woman who was a regular attendee at the feasts was expecting to give birth imminently. Her husband was a poorly paid porter, and they already had five children.

"You have enough children to feed now, without adding to your financial burden," the judge's wife said to her. "I'm not able to have children. If you let me raise this child, I promise I will care for it as if it were my own. And if you keep our arrangement a secret, I will support you and your family for the rest of your lives."

134

The woman agreed. When the child was born, she handed him over to the judge's wife. That morning, the servant was given a longer shopping list than usual. It included beans, peas, white haricots, cabbage, lentils, onions, garlic, a variety of heavy grains, and spices. An expert cook, who had prepared all the dishes which she had claimed came from her generous relatives, the wife knew perfectly well what effect the carefully selected foods would have on one's digestion.

It had been a hard day's work for the judge, and his capacious stomach was feeling emptier than usual. He was overjoyed at the sight of the exceptionally lavish feast, and he helped himself to a plate of everything, and then went through the menu again until the table was bare and his belly was stretched nearly to bursting point.

He lay back exhausted by his over-indulgence.

"Your relatives have outdone themselves, my dear," he said to his wife, congratulating himself once again on his wise choice of a mate. But after an hour, he could feel a deep rumbling from inside, and movements portending an earthquake. Sharp spasms like lightning strikes were accompanied by claps of thunder that grew louder, until he was sure the neighbours could hear them. His stomach swelled, and he fell to the floor and rolled around in agony.

"I have a storm inside me," he cried.

His wife came running with a tea made of fennel and anise – carminatives used to help expel intestinal gas that she had prepared earlier – and made him drink it while she massaged his belly. Suddenly, she stopped.

"Oh, my master," she exclaimed. "Praise be to Allah. It's a miracle!"

"What are you talking about, woman?" the judge groaned between spasms.

"Oh, my master, oh, my master! A miracle!" she repeated.

"Stop torturing me. What is happening?"

"My dear husband, I can feel it moving inside you. You're going to have a baby."

135

"A baby? How can a man have a baby?"

"Only Allah knows, praise be his name."

The internal growls and grumbles increased, and then a rich and resonant fart exploded from him, reverberating through the house and propelling him violently across the room. He fainted.

When he returned to consciousness, he saw his wife cooing and crooning over a baby boy on a mattress beside him. He remembered the pain and the pressure in his belly and the sudden relief, and the evidence before his eyes convinced him that he had indeed miraculously given birth.

"All things are possible with Allah," he said, feeling his chest. "But how can a man produce milk for an infant?"

"Fortunately, one of our neighbours has just had a baby, and she has enough milk for two. She has agreed to be his wet nurse. Now, after your exertions you need to rest, so go to sleep, my husband."

He slept, and when he woke up he was refreshed in body but uneasy in his mind.

"We must keep this miracle a secret," he said to his wife. "If word gets out that I've given birth, people with vicious minds will say that I had indulged in unnatural practices – I, their virtuous and respectable judge."

"I'm afraid it's not possible to keep it a secret," she replied, making an effort to appear sympathetic. "The nurse has told her friends and neighbours, and they have told their friends and neighbours, so the whole city will probably have the news by now."

"I'm ruined. I don't know what to do."

"There will be plenty of time to decide. You need to stay in bed for forty days to recover."

The judge was a changed man during his extended postpartum period. Deeply mortified, he brooded silently, and when he spoke it was to make polite requests instead of giving abrupt orders. There was no more talk of laying the gold-fringed cloth. When his wife gave him permission to leave his bed at the end of his lying-in, he announced his decision.

"I can't stay here. No one will respect me. My reputation is destroyed."

"Yes, I agree that is for the best," said his wife. "You know that I will miss you, my dear master, but perhaps you can return in the future when everyone has forgotten."

He sneaked out of the city at night and made his way to Damascus, where he thought no one would recognize him or know of his story. However, in the shops and markets and cafés he heard endless tales and gossip of the judge in Tarabulus who had given birth. To the bare story were added scurrilous details of the event and slanderous allegations of activities whose names he dared not put into words. But at least he took comfort in the fact that no one knew his face. He had taken some money with him and lived frugally, shedding the excess weight he had accumulated over the past year. But eventually the money ran out, and he had to sell his fine clothes. He considered sending a message to his wife asking her to send some of his cached gold coins, but that meant he would have to tell her where his treasure was concealed, so he swallowed his pride and hired himself out as a common labourer.

After many years, when he had become as gaunt as a street dog, he felt he might safely return to Tarabulus, where no one would recognize him as their prosperous judge and they should have forgotten about the scandal. As he entered the city, he saw a group of boys playing. One of them jeered at another, "How do you expect to win, when you were born in the year of the judge, the Father of Farts?"

The judge smiled with relief. Some other judge had apparently disgraced himself by farting in public, and that event had driven the memory of his own misfortune out of the people's minds. Expecting an amusing story, he asked the boy, "Who is the judge you spoke of, and why is he called the Father of Farts?"

"Many years ago, this judge let off a tremendous fart, and his wife convinced him that ..."

When the boy finished, the judge understood and almost admired his wife's elaborate deceit, and it dawned on him why she had carried out her vengeful design. He rushed to his house to find nothing but a roofless ruin and all the furniture gone, except the cabinet, which was empty.

The neighbours heard his howl of anguish, and they came and told him, with a thin show of sympathy, that his wife had given him up for dead and had packed all the contents of the house and departed for a far-off country.

The judge left Tarabulus and was never heard of again.

ST J2321.2. Man thinks he has given birth to a child by letting wind.

Five Eggs
Spain (also Ecuador, Portugal, Middle East)

Marta sent her husband, Martín, to the market to buy eggs. He found that he had only enough money for five. When he arrived home he said:

"Marta, boil these eggs – three for me and two for you."

"Ah, no," she said. "I get three and you get two."

"But I'm the one who went to the market and brought them home. I get three."

"And I'm the one who is cooking them. I get three."

The argument continued while the eggs boiled. Finally, Martín said, "If I don't get three, I'll leave."

"Go ahead and leave. If I don't get three, I'll die."

"Go ahead and die, then."

Marta fell to the floor and lay as if dead.

Martín knew that she was spoofing.

"Good. Now I get all five."

"Three for me," Marta whispered.

"Well, I'll just have to make a coffin and tell our neighbours that you're dead and ask them to help me bury you."

He built a coffin and placed Marta in it, and then went to announce her death to the neighbours. Four of them carried the coffin to the cemetery. Martín walked alongside, wailing and sobbing, "My poor Marta. What will I do without her? If only she had agreed that I get three and she gets two."

"Three for me," came the voice from the coffin.

They arrived at the cemetery and lowered the coffin into the grave.

"This is your last chance," Martín whispered to the coffin.

"Three for me," she answered.

Martín started to nail the lid on the coffin. Marta suddenly leapt out of the grave, shouting, "All right. You can have three."

The neighbours thought she was really dead, and they took to their heels in fright. Marta and Martín walked back home and sat down at the table with the five eggs on a plate between them. Marta took one and started to eat it.

"I have to admit you made a beautiful coffin for me."

Martín started to eat his first egg.

"I have to admit you were a beautiful corpse."

Marta ate her second egg.

"Weren't the neighbours funny the way they were frightened?"

Martín ate his second egg.

"They'll have a story to tell their grandchildren."

Marta suddenly screamed and pointed behind Martín. When he turned to look, Marta grabbed the last egg and popped it into her mouth.

"And three for me," she said triumphantly.

Nasruddin Hodja and His Cousins
World-wide

"Nasruddin Hodja" means "Victory-of-Faith Master" and has a variety of spellings and local versions: Johah, Xuha, Juha, Guha, Cogia, Yehá. It is believed that he was a real person who lived in Turkey in the 13th century. Many of the same wise fool and trickster tales that have accumulated around him are also attributed to folklore characters in other countries, for example, Afantee, Perurimá, Pedro Urdemales, and in English-language traditions the ubiquitous Jack, represented below by Jonathan Swift's servant, whose real name was Alexander Magee, but who Swift called "Saunders", his generic name for a succession of servants. When Magee died at the age of 29 in 1721, Swift had him buried in Saint Patrick's Cathedral in Dublin with a plaque inscribed:

> Here lieth the body of Alexander Magee, servant to Doctor Swift, Dean of St. Patrick's. His grateful master caused this monument to be erected in memory of his discretion, fidelity, and diligence, in that humble station.

It is recommended that if you tell one Hodja story you should tell seven, because hearing seven Hodja tales takes one a further step toward enlightenment.

Hodja heard a man boasting that no one could trick him.

"Wait here," Hodja told him. "I'll find a way to trick you."

Hodja walked off. The man waited. And waited. A shopkeeper noticed that he had been standing there for quite some time.

"What are you doing here?" he asked.

"Nasruddin Hodja heard me say that no one can trick me. He told me he'd find a way. I'm waiting to see if he does."

"You can stop waiting."

"Why?"

"He already did."

Hodja was trying to take a nap, but the noise of children playing in the street kept him awake. He had an idea.

"Hey, boys and girls. Don't you know they're giving away fresh melons at the market on the other side of town?"

The children ran off. Hodja settled back for a nap. Soon he heard a lot of people running down the street. He went out to see what was happening.

"Hodja," one man said. "Don't you know they're giving away fresh melons at the market on the other side of town?"

"So maybe it's true," Hodja said to himself, and he joined the stampede.

Hodja was expecting a large number of guests for dinner and didn't have a pot big enough to cook for all of them, so he borrowed a big pot from a neighbour. He returned it the following day with a small pot inside.

"Hodja, why is the small pot inside my big one?"

"Oh, while your pot was with me it had a baby."

The neighbour said nothing and kept the small pot. A few weeks later, Hodja had another large dinner party and borrowed the neighbour's pot again. A week went by and he hadn't returned it. The neighbour came to him and said, "Hodja, where is the pot I loaned to you?"

"I'm sorry to say your pot died."

"Died? How can a pot die? I don't believe it."

"You believed that a pot could have a baby."

Hodja was an imam, a holy man whose job it was to preach sermons in the mosque. One Friday, Hodja had neglected to prepare a sermon. He stood in front of the people and said, "Do you know what I'm going to say to you?"

They said, "No."

"Well, I'm not going to waste my time speaking to such ignorant people," he said, and he walked out of the mosque.

The following Friday, he again had not prepared a sermon. He stood in front of the people and said, "Do you know what I'm going to say to you?"

The people, who had felt cheated the preceding week, said, "Yes."

"Well, since you already know, I'm not going to waste my time telling you." And he walked out of the mosque.

Again the next Friday he was unprepared. He said to the people, "Do you know what I'm going to say to you?"

The people said, "Some of us do and some of us don't."

"Well, those who do can tell those who don't." And he walked out of the mosque.

Cogia Efendi one day went into a garden, pulled up some carrots and turnips and other kinds of vegetables, which he found, putting some into a sack and some into his bosom; suddenly the gardener coming up, laid hold of him, and said, "What are you seeking here?"

The Cogia, being in great consternation, not finding any other reply, answered, "For some days past a great wind has been blowing, and that wind blew me hither."

"But who pulled up these vegetables?" said the gardener.

"As the wind blew very violently," replied the Cogia, "it cast me here and there, and whatever I laid hold of in the hope of saving myself remained in my hands."

"Ah," said the gardener, "but who filled the sack with them?"

"Well," said the Cogia, "that is the very question I was about to ask myself when you came up."

(George Borrow, *The Turkish Jester*, 1884)

Yehá was invited by a group of young men to go to the baths with them. They each carried a concealed egg, because they planned to play a trick on Yehá. When they had disrobed and were in the water, one of them said,

"Let's all lay an egg. Whoever can't do it will pay the cost of the baths."

One by one they imitated a clucking hen and produced an egg in their hands.

Yehá stood in front of them and went, "Cock-a-doodle-doo."

"What are you doing, Yehá?" they said.

"Have you ever seen a flock of chickens without a rooster?"

Yehá thought it was about time he settled his bill at the vegetable shop.

"How much do I owe you?" he asked the shopkeeper.

The shop keeper opened his account book. Yehá saw that he owed 31 *reales*, and he noticed that the local imam owed 26 reales.

"Look, my friend," he said. "I owe you 31 reales, and the imam owes you 26, making the difference five reales. So if you pay me the five reales, your books will be balanced."

The shop keeper thought for a moment and said, "That's a good idea, Yehá. Here you are."

As Yehá walked off with the five reales, the shop keeper congratulated himself on clearing up two debts at once, but after pondering the matter for a while, he was not sure that it was such a good idea after all.

The landlord says that Abbot and Costello owe seven weeks' room rent at $13 a week. Costello insists that he paid it in full: $28. He proves that seven goes into 28 thirteen times, but the explanation is beyond my capacity to explain, so you will have to see it on YouTube at "Abbott & Costello - 7x13 = 28".

J2213. Illogical use of numbers.

Many years ago, when I was teaching English to foreigners in Dublin, two young Chinese women, Jun and Cindy, with only a rudimentary grasp of the language, managed to present these two stories to the class, after much discussion in Chinese and beeping of their electronic Chinese-English dictionaries.

A rich man owned a large tree next to his house, and he was annoyed that the poor people sat in its shade during the hottest part of the day, so he told the people they couldn't use the shade unless they paid him. The people asked Afantee, champion of the poor, for help. Afantee bought the shade from the rich man and allowed the poor people to use it any time they wished. Of course, as the sun moved across the sky the shade moved and the people moved with it. When the shade moved to the rich man's garden, the people followed it. The rich man complained, but Afantee pointed out that he now owned the shade, and the man couldn't do anything about it.

A poor young man wanted to marry the daughter of a rich man, but the rich man refused permission unless the young man gave him a gift, which the young man couldn't afford to do. He brought his problem to Afantee, who shoved a gold coin up his donkey's bottom and gave the donkey to the young man with instructions on what to do when he gave it to the rich man. He brought the donkey to the rich man and told him that it produced gold coins. He demonstrated by giving the donkey a kick in the ribs, which made the animal expel the coin. The girl's father was pleased and gave his permission for the marriage.

The Chilean trickster Pedro Urdemales played that trick on the king.

K111.1. Alleged gold-dropping animal sold.

Jonathan Swift, author of *Gulliver's Travels* and other classic works, and dean of Saint Patrick's Cathedral in Dublin, liked his food. One evening, his servant Jack was cooking a goose for the dean and, being hungry, ate one of the legs. When he set the goose on the table, Swift said, "Jack, there's only one leg. Did you eat the other one?"

"No, sir. This sort of goose has only one leg."

"I don't believe that, Jack."

The following day, they were driving in the country when they came to a lake where geese were standing one-legged in the shallow water.

"See, sir, that's the breed of goose I served last night – only one leg."

Swift ran toward the geese shouting "Hoosh!" The geese took flight, revealing two legs.

"So, Jack, two legs. What do you say to that?"

"You didn't hoosh the goose last night, sir."

K402.1. The goose without a leg. Accused of eating the goose's leg, the thief maintains that it had no leg, and cleverly enforces his point by showing geese standing on one leg. (Usually the master confounds the rascal by frightening the geese so that they use both legs.)

This is in Boccaccio's 14th-century *Decameron*, Day VI, novel 4, and in Tarlton's *Newes out of Purgatorie* (c. 1590), under the title of "The Tale of the Cook, and why he sat in Purgatorie with a Crane's Leg in his Mouth". Jesucristo and San Pedro are the characters in a Yaqui Indian version.

The Inconstant Widow
China

(Mostly paraphrased and quoted from Du Halde's *Description of the Empire of China and Chinese-Tartary*, 1741, with quotes in italics)

In the fourth century BC there lived in China a famous philosopher named Chwang Tze (Master Chwang), who was a disciple of Lao Tzu, the founder of Taoism. As Zhuangzi – his name is spelled variously – he is credited with the authorship of one of the foundation texts of Taoism called the *Zhuangzi*. It is a compendium of teachings and stories, analogous to the Bible, and is one of the most influential works in Chinese literature. This typical parable from the book is frequently quoted. A ghost speaks:

145

Formerly, I, Kwang Kâu, dreamt that I was a butterfly, a butterfly flying about, feeling that it was enjoying itself. It did not know that it was Kâu. Suddenly I awoke, and was myself again, the veritable Kâu. I did not know whether it had formerly been Kâu dreaming that he was a butterfly, or it was now a butterfly dreaming that it was Kâu. But between Kâu and a butterfly there must be a difference. This is a case of what is called the Transformation of Things.

He perfectly comprehended the difference between what is visible and invisible; between the body, which is corruptible, and the spirit, which leaving that abode acquires new life by a kind of wonderful transformation.

Chwang Tze was married three times. His first wife died, and he divorced his second for infidelity. His third wife, Tyen, was of royal blood. She was well-shaped, beautiful, witty, sweet and vivacious, and he loved her dearly.

He was invited by the king of Tzu to be his prime minister, but he gently turned down the offer with this story.

A heifer destined for sacrifice, decorated in the fine ornaments of a victim, was being led in a formal procession to the temple. She passed a team of oxen sweating at the plough, and the sight made her feel proud and superior. However, when she arrived at the temple and saw the sacrificial knife raised to kill her, she wished she could trade places with the sweating oxen she had despised.

Chwang Tze retired to the mountains with his third wife, so he could live in peaceful contemplation of nature and enjoy the pleasures of the countryside. One day, as he was walking and meditating, he came upon a cemetery. Strolling among the graves and reflecting on the equal status in death of all those who had been rich or poor, wise or ignorant in life, he noticed a newly erected tomb on a small mound of fresh clay that was still moist. A young lady clad in a white sackcloth robe of mourning was fanning the top of the mound with a white fan.

"May I ask why you are fanning the soil?" Chwang Tze politely inquired.

"This is the tomb of my beloved husband," she replied. "We were very close. He made me promise on his deathbed that I wouldn't marry again until the earth on his grave was dry. I'm just helping it along."

Chwang Tze managed to suppress his laughter. He wondered to himself: if she loved him so much, what would she have done if she had hated him?

"The clay is very damp," he said to her. "It will take a long time for you to dry it that way. Permit me to help you."

She accepted his offer and gave him a white fan like the one she was using. *Then Chwang Tze, who had the art of raising spirits, called them to his assistance, and striking the tomb with the fan, immediately all the moisture disappeared.* The lady offered him a silver bodkin and the white fan in gratitude. He refused the bodkin but accepted the fan. *The lady withdrew well satisfied, joy appearing both in her countenance and gesture.*

Chwang Tze reflected on the inconstancy of women as he walked home. He sat in the hall gazing at the white fan. He sighed and, thinking he was alone, composed a poem and spoke it aloud.

> A grieving widow mourns with glee.
> I can see that it is clear:
> The man is treated shabbily
> By the one he held most dear.

However, his wife, Tyen, was standing behind him.

"Why are you sighing and where did you get that fan?" she said.

As he related the incident, Tyen's face grew red with indignation. When he finished, she said angrily, *"She is the reproach of mankind, the scandal of her sex, a monster of insensibility. Is it possible to find such a vile heart as hers?"*

Still bemused and shocked by the widow's behaviour, he ignored his wife and composed another poem.

> While he's alive she flatters her man.
> As soon as he's dead, she takes a white fan
> And dries off his grave, for this is her plan –
> To marry again as soon as she can.

Tyen's response to that was to get even angrier.

"How have you the boldness to speak after this manner in my presence, to condemn all women and confound so unjustly those who are virtuous with wretches that do not deserve to live? Are you not ashamed to pass such an unjust sentence? And are you not afraid to be punished for it?"

"Tell me then, my dear, if I were to die now, with you beautiful and in the prime of life, would you spend even three years, as our culture demands, before thinking of taking a new husband?"

"No. A virtuous widow never thinks of a second husband. I would never marry again for the rest of my life, let alone three years."

"Promises are easy to make but hard to keep," Chwang Tze said calmly. That threw her into an even greater passion. She spoke at length, but this is the gist:

"We women are nobler and more constant than you men. What sort of example are you? You married soon after your first wife died, and you divorced your second wife. Why are you torturing me like this?"

She grabbed the white fan and tore it to shreds.

"It is gratifying to see you worked up over this matter," said Chwang Tze. That appeased her, and they changed the subject.

148

A few days later, Chwang Tze fell seriously ill. Tyen sighed and wept continually and never left his bedside.

"I think I'm going to die today or tomorrow," he said. "It's a pity you destroyed that white fan. You'd find it useful to dry the cement on my tomb."

"Don't be so suspicious," she said. "It's upsetting to you and hurtful to me. I swear I'll never give my heart to another."

"I'm convinced of your constancy," he said, and he died.

Tyen shrieked with grief and embraced his corpse. Then she laid him out and placed him in his coffin in the main hall and dressed in mourning. The neighbours and his admirers from far away came to pay their respects, among them Wang Sun, a young, handsome, well-dressed man who claimed to be descended from the king of Tzu, the king who had invited Chwang Tze to be his prime minister.

"Years ago," he said to Tyen, "I told Chwang Tze that I wanted to be his student, and the reason I came now was to study with him. What a disappointment to learn that he is dead! I will look for convenient lodging nearby so I can stay for the hundred-day mourning period while I read his works."

He took off his fine clothes and dressed in a mourning robe. Tyen was immediately attracted to him, and she accommodated him and his serving man in a room off the main hall. Whenever the widow came into the hall to weep over the coffin, which happened often, Wang Sun would come out of his room to speak with her. These frequent interviews soon included fond glances, and Tyen was glad that the other mourners had left and few visitors came to the house. It was not proper for a woman to make the first advances, so she sent for Wang Sun's servant and plied him with wine and questions: was Wang Sun married – no – then what qualities did he look for in a wife?

"I have heard him say that if he could meet with one like you, it would be the height of his wishes."

"Speak of me to him, and if you find that he likes me, assure him that I shall look upon it as the greatest happiness to be his."

"There is no need of sounding his inclinations, because he has told me that such a marriage would be entirely agreeable to his taste, but that he thought it impracticable, at least indecent, as he was a disciple of the deceased."

"That's not a problem. He was never actually a student; he only wanted to become one."

She sent the servant on his way, telling him to let her know as soon as he had his master's reply, regardless of the time night or day. The following day he told her:

"My master says that there are three insuperable obstacles: one, the wedding can't be held in the hall, because the coffin is there; two, he is worried that your heart will remain with your late husband and will never be his; and three, he can't afford the costs of the wedding."

"Those obstacles can easily be removed. One: what is the coffin but a box with a stinking carcass? I'll have it moved into an old ruin of a house nearby. Two: my late husband was not as great as his reputation; he refused the king of Tsu's invitation to be prime minister because he knew he was not capable of the job. Also, he was not kind to me. We quarrelled recently over an incident in which he helped a widow dry her husband's tomb with a fan, which he kept as a reminder of her kindness. Three: I have enough money to pay for the wedding and new clothes for your master.

"Tell him that as we are both of the nobility, and it is fortuitous that we have met just now when we are both available, it is obviously the will of Heaven that we be married."

The servant took this message to his master, who agreed, and then conveyed that decision to the widow. She was so overjoyed that she immediately cast off her mourning clothes and dressed in her finest attire and adornments, and had the coffin removed to the old house and ordered the wedding feast to be prepared.

After the feast, they had just entered the nuptial chamber when Wang Sun suddenly fell to the floor in convulsions. Tyen asked him what was wrong, but he was in such agony he couldn't speak. She shouted for help, and the servant came running.

"Has he had fits like this before?" she asked.

"Barely a year goes by when he doesn't, and there is only one remedy. The royal physician discovered that the brain of a recently deceased person mixed with wine will bring the convulsions to an immediate end."

"I know just where to find such a brain," she said, and she took a hatchet in one hand and a lamp in the other and ran to the old ruined house.

A woman's strength would normally not be enough to chop through the lid of a coffin, but this lid was not a normal one. Chwang Tze, being fond of life and having heard that people had been buried alive, had ordered that the lid be made of very thin wood so he could break it if necessary. The lid split at Tyen's first blow, and a few more finished the job. Pausing to catch her breath before harvesting the brain of her late husband, she heard a sigh from the coffin. To her horror, she saw Chwang Tze sit up. She dropped the hatchet in shock.

Chwang Tze stepped out of the coffin and picked up the lamp and walked toward the house. Tyen followed him, sweating and trembling in dread anticipation of what would happen when he found Wang Sun and his servant in the bedroom. When she and Chwang Tze arrived, she was relieved to see that they were not there. Casting a kind look on Chwang Tze, she said:

"Your little slave has done nothing night and day since you died but think of you. At length hearing a noise proceed from the coffin, and calling to mind stories I have been told of dead people returning to life, I flattered myself that you might be of this number, so I ran as fast as I could to open the coffin, and thanks be to Heaven, my hopes are not deceived. What a happiness it is to me to regain my dear, whose loss I continually bewailed!"

"I am obliged to you," replied Chwang Tze, *"for such extraordinary affection to me. I have, however, one short question to ask you: why are you not in mourning, and how come you to be dressed in a rich brocade?"*

The answer was ready. "As I went," said she, *"to open your coffin with a secret foreboding of my happiness, the joy I ought to have on that occasion did not require a melancholy dress, nor was it fitting to receive you alive in a mourning habit, for which reason I put on my wedding clothes."*

"But why was my coffin placed in the old house and not in the hall where it ought to have been?"

The lady could think of no response to that. Chwang Tze gazed at the food and drink and provisions for the feast. He asked for hot wine and drank several glasses without speaking. Then he composed these verses:

> If I consent to live with you
> As a husband ought to do,
> I fear that you might come again
> With an axe to take my brain,
> Much more eager for a man
> Than the widow with the fan.

Then he pointed behind her and said, "Who are those two men?"

She turned around and saw Wang Sun and his servant entering the house. She was terrified, but when she turned to look again they were gone. She went away and hanged herself out of shame. Chwang Tze found her and placed her in his mended coffin, smashed all the crockery and burned the house to the ground, cremating Tyen's body.

Chwang Tze set off to travel, determined never to marry again. He eventually met up with his master, Lao Tzu, and remained with him for the rest of his life.

H466. Feigned death to test wife's faithfulness.

K2213.1. Matron of Ephesus.

The motif is generally known as The Widow of Ephesus, from the version in the first-century AD *Satyricon*, chapters 111 and 112, by Petronius Arbiter, which can be summarized thus:

A woman mourned in the tomb of her deceased husband for five days without eating or drinking. Thieves were crucified nearby with a soldier on guard to prevent relatives from taking the bodies for burial. The soldier heard the woman's loud wailing and went to investigate and persuaded her to eat and drink. With that need satisfied, she took an interest in the soldier, and they quickly became lovers. Relatives took advantage of the soldier's absence and removed a body. The soldier would be executed if the loss was discovered, so the woman offered her husband's body as a substitute, saying, "I would rather make a dead man useful, than send a live man to death."

A literary protégée of Jonathan Swift wrote a version of The Widow of Ephesus, in which Swift and his servant Jack argue about the constancy of women. They see a widow grieving at her just-deceased husband's grave. Jack, to prove his point that women are unfaithful, proposes to her, saying that his chaplain is in the coach and can marry them immediately. She accepts.

Irish Highwaymen, Tories and Rapparees

Most of the following stories are included in the 1776 edition of John Cosgrave's sensational and controversial *A Genuine History of the Lives and Actions of the Most Notorious Irish Highwaymen, Tories and Rapparees*, which first appeared in 1747 and then in many subsequent editions and printings. The author attempted to pre-empt accusations of romanticizing criminal activity by explaining in three separate places in the book:

"I have wrote with no other design than to discourage young men from falling into such company as may lead them into a shameful way of living, which often brings them to an ill end, and leaves a reproach upon their family, who may be innocent."

"... our intent in publishing this history is only to put honest people on their guard against robbers and rogues ..."

"If I can shew an honest man how to outwit a rogue, or put a trick on him, 'tis as much as can be expected; and verily that was my chief design in publishing this book."

Many of these outlaws were from prosperous families who had lost their properties after failed rebellions or as retribution for siding with King James in the 1688-91 war against the pretender William of Orange. They had no option but to support themselves and defend the oppressed poor by robbing the rich. Although the men whose lives Cosgrave documents all came to sticky ends, his treatment of their actions is non-judgemental and, in fact, appears to be at least mildly celebratory.

William Carleton, in his 1862 historical novel *Redmond Count O'Hanlon, the Irish Rapparee*, certainly glorified his heroes. He intriguingly commented: "Now, most of these men have personal records left of their lives and deaths. They held high but subordinate appointments under their celebrated chief [O'Hanlon], and such of them as have not distinct biographies, are incidentally mentioned by their clever and graphic biographer, Cosgrave, who was himself their contemporary, and if we are to be guided by a hint in what purports to be a letter to him evidently written, however, by himself, there is reason to suppose that he was one of their fraternity."

Redmond O'Hanlon

The N1 between Dundalk in the Republic of Ireland and Newry in Northern Ireland, a distance of 15 miles (24km), runs through a narrow, claustrophobic glen called the Moyry Pass. Also known as the Gap of the North, it is infamous as a place of ambush and defence in legend and history. It's one of the passes where Cúchulainn defended Ulster against Maeve's armies in the epic *Táin Bó Cuailnge* (The Cattle Raid of Cooley), and the English came to grief here more than once. It was also one of the favourite haunts of the notorious and elusive 17th-century highwayman Redmond O'Hanlon (c. 1641-1681), of whom it was said: "There was plenty of him where he could be spared, and the greatest possible scarcity where he was wanted."

The O'Hanlon family lost their property near Slieve Gullion, next to the Moyry Pass, in the aftermath of the 1641 rebellion. Redmond was accused of being present at the killing of a gentleman – one source says members of his gang committed the deed in his absence – and he went on the run to avoid arrest and was outlawed. So he became a rapparee, forced to live outside the law of an oppressive government. Many of Cosgrave's stories about him are still in circulation, partly due to Carleton's fictionalized treatment.

O'Hanlon was riding along the Moyry Pass looking for prey when he came across a pedlar who complained that he had just been beaten and robbed by "that damned rogue of a Redmond O'Hanlon". Indignant that someone would rob in his name, O'Hanlon caught the robber, put him into the hands of the pedlar, made the pedlar promise to prosecute him, and wrote out a sort of citizen's arrest document called a *mittimus*, which read:

"By Redmond O Hanlon, *in loco* of one of his Majesty's justices of the peace for the said county [Armagh], but chief ranger of the mountains, I herewith send you ... etcetera."

This "gave rise to as pleasant a fit of merriment in court as ever happened upon such an occasion, the judges and everyone else laughing till they were ready to burst, at the conceit of Redmond acting the justice of peace."

One day, dressed as usual in the garb of a well-to-do gentleman, O'Hanlon requested a squad of soldiers from Armagh to accompany him, as he was carrying a significant amount of money and was worried that Redmond O'Hanlon might rob him. He led them to a place where he had stationed some of his gang, and then told the soldiers that he felt he was past the point of danger. He paid them off and asked them to fire their weapons to celebrate the success of their task. They fired repeatedly at his request until they had exhausted their ammunition. Then O'Hanlon called for his men, who robbed and stripped the soldiers.

In Carleton's largely fictional *Redmond*, O'Hanlon rescues a young woman kidnapped by a thuggish army officer, Lucas, steals £300 from his desk, and then lures him into a trap. He has a confederate send a message to Lucas that he is wounded in an inn, Four Mile House, between Newry and Dundalk. Lucas and twelve dragoons go there only to be told that O'Hanlon has not arrived but is expected shortly. The soldiers are plied with drink while they wait and then are made to go outside while a "dying woman" is tended to by an elderly "clergyman" – O'Hanlon in disguise – who just "happened" to be passing by.

"Retire with quietness, soldiers," he tells them. "Never mind the arms; the noise of removing them will distract and disturb her at this solemn moment, when all should be peace."

This gives the innkeeper the opportunity to water the powder of their firearms. Having calmed and reassured the woman with his prayers, the clergyman places a sum of

156

money into the hands of the landlord for her care. This is presumably the money he had stolen from Lucas' desk. Eventually, Lucas realizes that O'Hanlon is not going to show up, and he and his men set off for their barracks in Armagh, accompanied by the "clergyman" at his request for his protection. A motley group of men who had been in the inn have mysteriously disappeared. Some miles from the inn, in a lonely and narrow part of the road, the soldiers are confronted by O'Hanlon's band. The soldiers try to shoot, but "nothing resulted but so many flashes in the pan." They are quickly overpowered and stripped, and Lucas is tied to a tree at O'Hanlon's order and given fifty lashes with a cat-o-nine-tails before they are made to walk back to their barracks.

But events didn't always turn out the way O'Hanlon planned. A Dundalk merchant who was owed £200 (about £30,000 in today's money) by a merchant in Newry was looking for a way to get the cash through the Moyry Pass without it falling into O'Hanlon's hands. His young apprentice, a picture of slow-witted innocence, volunteered to collect it. The merchant had serious doubts, but the boy promised to forfeit his ears if he failed. The merchant agreed, and the boy asked him for a bag of forty shillings worth of ha'pennies, which he put into both ends of a sack so he could sling it over the saddle. The merchant offered him a good horse, but the boy selected the most decrepit old nag he could find, "so lame with the spavy [spavin, caused by osteoarthritis] that he could hardly go a mile an hour, and, what was worse than all, the brute, from sheer viciousness and a hellfire temper, would suffer neither horse nor man to come near him on the road, the apprentice himself being the only person he would allow to handle or mount him" (Carleton, *Redmond*).

The boy set off for Newry with the bag of ha'pennies tucked inside his shirt, and before long he met up with Redmond O'Hanlon dressed as a gentleman and mounted on a fine horse. The rapparee greeted the boy in a friendly manner and asked him his business. The boy told him, and O'Hanlon asked when he planned to return to Dundalk.

"About this time tomorrow," the boy said ingenuously.

O'Hanlon gave him a penny to drink his health and warned him not to discuss his business with strangers.

The following day, the boy collected the £200 in notes and sewed them safely inside his waistcoat, slinging the bag of ha'pennies over the saddle. On his return through Moyry Pass, O'Hanlon met him and asked if he had the money with him. The boy said he had it in gold coins, and indicated the bag of ha'pennies.

"If you let me look at it, I'll count it to make sure it's all there," said O'Hanlon.

"It's all there," said the boy. "I counted it myself. And besides, I promised my master that I wouldn't let it into anyone's hands but my own."

O'Hanlon demanded that he give it to him. The boy refused, saying his master would think he took it himself. O'Hanlon produced a gun and threatened to shoot if the boy did not hand it over.

"I can't do that. I told my master that he could cut my ears off if I didn't bring the money back."

(The boy probably knew that O'Hanlon prided himself on the fact that he had never killed anyone.)

O'Hanlon approached to try to grab the sack, but the boy's horse lunged and kicked out at him, forcing him to keep his distance.

The boy threw the bag of ha'pennies over the hedge into a bog saying, "If you want it, then follow it."

O'Hanlon dismounted and tied his horse to a tree. When the rapparee was well inside the bog, the boy jumped off his old nag and onto O'Hanlon's fine fast horse and galloped to Dundalk.

The honest merchant advertised the "found" horse. No one claimed it, but he received an unsigned letter stating that the owner of the horse made a present of it to the boy "in reward for his cleverness and ingenuity".

Although O'Hanlon was credited with many cunning and lucky escapes, he met his end at the hands of a trusted kinsman tempted by the £400 reward offered by the government.

K2378.4. Ammunition saved till enemy has used his.

The Tipperary rapparee Edmond O'Ryan (1670-1724) also played this trick. He is said to have composed the still-popular Irish song, "Éamonn an Chnoic" (Ned of the Hill), which describes his isolation from his sweetheart and friends because of his outlaw status.

Billy Peters and Cathair na gCapall

Billy's real name was William Delany (hanged 1737), and Cathair's real name was Charles Dempsey (hanged 1735). Both were from County Laois. "Cathair" is an Irish variant of Charles, and "na gCapall" means "of the horses". He was a horse-whisperer and noted horse thief and finder of "lost" horses. There is a street named Cathair na gCapall in Portarlington, County Laois, where he is a well-known figure of local legend and history.

Carleton's *Redmond Count O'Hanlon* has a scene in which a number of rapparees exchange yarns while awaiting their leader's arrival.

> "Come, Billy Peters, or whatsomever you call yourself, let us hear a little of your skill and experience. You're nearly as great a horse stealer as Cahir na Cappul here."
>
> "Troth, the story I'm going to tell," replied Peters, "is as much Cahir na Cappul's as it is mine. But such as it is you shall have it."
>
> "Aye, do," said Cahir. "Tell it up for the gentlemen."
>
> "It so happened that I took a strong fancy to a fine sorrel stallion with a bald face and a white foot that belonged to a gentleman in the county of Carlow. I got into the stable one night by means of a thing that I'm sure none of you ever heard of: a false key. It isn't, nor ever was, my custom to do a thing unfairly, so, says I, whispering to the horse, 'Have you any objection to come with me and see the world?' Troth, I thought it

159

but fair and reasonable to put the question to him, but, at any rate, devil a word he said against it. 'That's all right,' says I. 'Silence gives consent,' and off we went on the best of terms with each other.

"Well, I sold the horse at a good price, but the pursuit soon caught up with me, and in a short time I was lodged in Carlow jail with every proof strong against me, so that I saw clearly there was little else for me but to dance the pleasant jig called the 'Hangman's Hornpipe'. Not that I was much troubled about that either, in regard as I was once hanged before and escaped the noose twice afterwards, and all by reason of a charm I got against hanging from the same woman that gave Cahir na Cappul there the enchantment that enables him, with a weeshy whisper in his ear, to tame the wildest and wickedest horse that ever went upon four feet.

"I sent to Cahir to let him know how I was fixed. I desired him to look at the stallion and to find me a mare as like him as possible, and try and exchange the one for the other; otherwise I had no chance. Ah, troth, Cahir my boy, it's you that wasn't long getting me the mare I wanted, nor in giving instructions how to have the thing done.

"The trial was now within a day or two of coming on, and the stolen horse was put under the care of the jailer, as is usual, till it should be over. When Cahir's messenger arrived, he put up at a place near the river where the hostler used to water the horse. He had got acquainted with him, and on this occasion asked him in to have a drink, to which he willingly consented, leaving the horse at the door. In the meantime, the horses were exchanged by a comrogue of the messenger's, and when the hostler came out he mounted the mare and rode her back to the stable instead of the stallion.

"Well, very soon afterwards my trial came on, and everything went against me. Nothing could be clearer

160

than the evidence, and the judge was going to charge the jury, when I thought it was time to speak.

"'My lord,' I said. 'Every man's life is precious to him. You all think me guilty, but I deny it and will prove my innocence if you grant me one request.'

"'What is it?' asked the judge.

"'That the horse shall be produced in court. When he is, if I don't show the whole world that I'm wrongfully charged with the crime I'm in for, why then, hang me up as an example to all the horse stealers in the kingdom, and I'll go to my death willingly.'

"'But how could the production of the horse save you?'

"'My lord, I cannot tell you that till the horse comes into the court.'

"'Very well,' said the judge, smiling. 'Let the horse be produced in court.'

"'The horse is my witness, my lord,' says I, 'and will bring me out clear.'

"'It is the first time I ever heard of such a witness,' said the judge, laughing outright, as did the whole court, 'but if you think he'll serve you, it is but right that you should have his testimony.'

"'We shall cross-examine him severely,' said the opposite counsel, 'and it'll go hard or we'll make him break down.'

"By this time the whole court was in roars of laughter, and they were all on coals to see what would happen. Well, in a short time the stallion was brought into the court, and I turned to the complainant.

"'Now, sir,' says I, 'do you swear positively and truly that that is the animal you lost?'

"'I do,' says he. 'By virtue of my oath, that is my horse, the very one you stole from me.'

"'By the virtue of your oath, sir, is that animal a stallion or a mare?'

"'By the oath I've taken, it's a stallion and not a mare. It was a stallion I lost, and that's the animal.'

161

"The short and the long of it was that the animal proved to be a mare. Such a scene was never witnessed. Everyone in the court was in convulsions, with the exception of the complainant, who had a face on him as long as today and tomorrow. As for the jury, you could have tied them with three straws.

"'Gentlemen,' says the judge, addressing them as well as he could speak for laughing, 'you must acquit the prisoner.'

"'We do, my lord,' said the foreman. 'We find a verdict of acquittal.'

"'Let him be immediately discharged, then,' said the judge.

"And so I was, comrades, and here I am."

"Give Peters a glass for that," said Patchy. "If that wasn't doing them, I don't know what was."

"But, sure, as I told you all, it was Cahir na Cappul here that deserves the credit. For what do you think he did? Why, he painted the mare so like the stallion that living eyes couldn't tell the difference."

Patrick Fleming

Fleming was raised by poor parents in Athlone, where his education extended little beyond learning to read and write. As a young man, he was a servant to the Earl of Antrim. A priest who was rumoured to have consorted with women lived in the house. One day when the priest was in a profound sleep, Patrick took a calf into his bedroom and wrote on the wall: "Woe be to you whoremongers." The calf was being weaned, and had been taught to take milk from Patrick's fingers.

(Watching a calf nurse at the teat of its mother does not adequately convey the desperate insistence of the sucking and the power of the massaging tongue when one inserts a milky finger into its mouth. It has to be experienced to be appreciated.)

162

Patrick uncovered the priest and put his "bauble" into the mouth of the calf, which "began to lug so hard that he awakened the priest, who in a very great surprise put out his hand to feel what had got hold of him." The calf had climbed on to the bed, and when the priest felt the cloven hoof, he was convinced that the Devil had come to pay him a visit.

He let out a roar for help, calling for holy water to repel the supposed demon. This brought the maids to investigate. When they saw what was happening they ran off screaming. Now the young ladies of the house came to the priest's room. He was praying and crossing himself, trying to escape from the calf, which stubbornly refused to give up the "teat". A brave servant managed to pull the calf away, and when the cause of the uproar was finally revealed, all burst out laughing. Patrick made the mistake of boasting to a fellow servant that he was the author of the trick. The servant informed the master, and Patrick was dismissed.

When he left, he took £400 worth of silverware and money with him, which was the beginning of his short career as a prolific robber, kidnapper and murderer. His end came in an inn near Maynooth in County Kildare. The innkeeper informed the authorities for the £100 reward, warning them that Fleming had fourteen members of his gang around him for protection. But the innkeeper's wife poured water into their firearms while they were drinking and carousing, wetting the powder and rendering the guns useless, so that when the sheriff and a strong guard surrounded the inn the outlaws were taken easily. Fleming was hanged near Dublin in 1650.

K633. Captor's powder is removed, ashes substituted: gun does not discharge.

The watered powder motif, also found in one of the Redmond O'Hanlon episodes, is probably best known from the ballad "Whiskey in the Jar":

163

I went up to my chamber, all for to take a slumber
I dreamt of gold and jewels and for sure it was no
　　wonder
But Jenny blew me charges and she filled them up
　　with water
Then sent for Captain Farrell to be ready for the
　　slaughter

It was early in the morning, just before I rose to travel
Up comes a band of footmen and likewise Captain
　　Farrell
I first produced me pistol for she stole away me rapier
I couldn't shoot the water, so a prisoner I was taken

The calf incident appears in the 1776 edition of
Cosgrave's *A Genuine History*. In at least one of the many
editions of the book, that element is censored, replaced
with "he got into the service of the earl of Antrim, where
he committed so many unlucky tricks, that a man would
be tired to rehearse the tenth part of them; he was soon
turned out of the earl's service."

Latin American Tricksters

The Caboclo and the Cheese
Brazil

The caboclo, a Brazilian trickster, is a complex character. He is of mixed European and Indian blood, and so neither one nor the other, an outsider with one foot in this world and the other in the world of spirits, a connection between humans and the gods. On the other hand, with its origins in slavery, the term caboclo historically carries a derogatory connotation, like the European "peasant". As a folklore personage, he can be a clever peasant or a wise fool, outwitting his social betters. This tale in a slightly different format appears as "A Loaf for a Dream" in the 14th-century Gesta Romanorum.

A priest, a student and a caboclo were travelling on a pilgrimage. Where they stopped one night there was no food, and all they had with them was one small piece of cheese, too small to share three ways.

The priest said, "Let's go to sleep. In the morning, the one who has had the most beautiful dream can eat the whole piece of cheese."

The caboclo woke up during the night and ate the cheese. In the morning, the priest said, "I had a beautiful dream. I was climbing Jacob's Ladder to Heaven."

The student said, "I dreamed I was already in Heaven waiting for you."

The caboclo said, "I dreamed that I saw you climbing Jacob's Ladder and meeting the student at the top and joining all your friends. I shouted, 'Hey, you two. You forgot the cheese.' And you said, 'We are in Heaven and don't need it. You can eat it.' So I ate it."

Pedro Urdemales
Chile

These two stories are translated from *Cuentos de Pedro Urdemales* (1925), collected from oral tradition by Ramón A. Laval, who tells us that Pedro was born in "a shack on the left bank of the River Maule [in Chile] on the night of 23 June 1701". He is the namesake of his illustrious Spanish ancestor who is the hero of the 1615 comedy by Cervantes, *Pedro de Urdemalas*, is mentioned in a 12th-century Aragonese document, and has been cited in Spanish dictionaries since 1595. He is the cousin of other Latin American Pedros with surnames such as Ordimán, Urdimal, Urdemalis, Malasartes, Undimales, Mal Urde, Ulimán, Animales, and Rimales, not forgetting the naturalized Paraguayan Perurimá, who took on a native Guaraní name.

On opening the door to his storeroom, the owner of a hacienda saw Pedro Urdemales calmly filling a sack with wheat. Pedro noticed him, but he continued with his task as if it were nothing unusual. The gentleman watched him for a while and then said, "What are you doing, man?"

"I don't answer nosy people," said Pedro coolly.

The gentleman let it go for the moment. Pedro finished filling the sack, tied the mouth closed, and hoisted it on to his shoulder without glancing at the owner.

"Well, my friend," said the gentleman sarcastically, "I hope that when you make tortillas you'll let me have one."

"I don't give to beggars," Pedro replied as he walked out the door nonchalantly.

Pedro robbed a traveller of two ounces of gold, which he changed into more than a thousand silver coins worth a quarter of a *real* each. (The price of a hen was two reales.) They were newly minted and shone like the sun. He poked holes in them with a small nail, ran threads through the holes, and hung them on a tree.

166

A gentleman riding along the road noticed the glittering "fruits" at a distance and spurred his horse on until he arrived and stared open-mouthed. He had never seen a tree that bore silver. Pedro was sitting in the shade with his back resting against the tree.

"Tell me, my friend," he said. "What kind of tree is this?"

"It's a silver tree," said Pedro.

"Sell me a shoot from it. I'll pay you a hundred pesos."

"Well, sir, I won't deceive you. The shoots from this tree don't grow."

"Then sell me the whole tree. I'll give you a thousand pesos for it."

"Sir, do you take me for a fool? How do you think I'd sell it to you for a thousand pesos, when it will produce much more than that in just one year?"

"I'll give you five thousand."

"No, your honour. Does your grace imagine that I'd give you such a bargain? If I were crazy enough to sell it, I wouldn't take a centavo less than ten thousand pesos."

The gentleman gave him ten thousand pesos and was well satisfied with the deal. But when he got home he realized that he had been tricked, and he rained down curses on the thief who had outwitted him.

Meanwhile, Pedro had gone to spend the money on wine, women and song.

Perurimá
Paraguay

"The East wind lies, because Perurimá comes from that direction."

Perurimá is a hero of the downtrodden victims of avaricious colonial oppressors: kings, priests, other representatives of authority, and the comfortably well-off in general. He represents the indigenous Guaraní way of life – *Ñande reko*: a constant search for an ideal world –

167

and reflects the aspiration of the underclass to get the better of their social superiors. Typical themes of the stories are one-upmanship, revenge and punishment generously seasoned with mockery and sarcasm.

He is known in Spain as Pedro de Urdemales and, to use a Spanish expression, he is as old as the itch. An immigrant who stowed away with the early conquistadors, he goes by various aliases in other Latin American countries. However, Perú (for short) is thoroughly naturalized and enthusiastically accepted by his adoptive folk culture, as authentically Paraguayan as *tereré*, the country's signature iced tea-like refreshment.

The following stories were collected from indigenous people, many of them monolingual – no Spanish and no English – in their own Guaraní language, and translated into Spanish, from which I have made these versions from two books by Miguelángel Meza, *Aventuras* and *Huellas* (see Sources).

Perurimá went to the house of the priest and said, "They tell me that nobody can play a trick on you. But I can."

"I don't think so," said the priest.

"All right, so I won't try. Goodbye."

"Wait. I'm going to visit a sick person. You can come along with me."

They started off, but the priest walked so fast that Perú was soon left behind, so he decided to stop and wait for the priest to return. While he was waiting, he noticed a large pile of fresh cow manure by the side of the road. He put his hat over it. Eventually, the priest came back.

"Why did you stay here?" the priest asked.

"I got so tired chasing a quail that I had to rest. I caught it, and it's there, under my hat."

"Wonderful," said the priest. "Now I have something to make my soup with."

To prevent the supposed bird from escaping, the priest carefully lifted the brim of the hat and quickly reached under it and grabbed a handful of the fresh manure.

One day Perurimá was standing by the side of a road in front of a building. When he saw the king approach on his horse, he went to lean against the wall. The king stopped in front of him and said, "Now, you son of the Devil, you're not going to make fun of me again."

"I bet I can," said Perú with a smile.

"What are you going to do to trick me?"

"Just come here and support this wall so it doesn't collapse, and I'll go and come back and trick you again."

The king dismounted and went to take Perú's place against the wall. Perú mounted the king's horse and galloped away.

(*Aventuras*)

The king decided that he had had enough of Perurimá's tricks, and one day he captured him, tied his hands and feet, and threw him into a dungeon guarded by two fierce dogs that could chew him to pieces. The following day, he took him out and said:

"Perurimá, I should close your eyes forever, but to show my benevolence, I'm going to give you one last chance. We're going to the seashore and throw stones. If you can throw a stone farther than I can, I'll let you go free. But if I throw one farther than you, I'll cut off your head with my own hands."

And he said to himself, "At last I have you, you son of a bad mother. I'm going to use a magic stone, and we'll see what you can do."

On their way to the sea, Perurimá pretended he had to defecate and stopped at a place where he knew there was a partridge nest. He picked up a young bird and put it in his pocket, making sure the king didn't notice.

When they arrived at the shore, the king made a running start and flung his magic stone. It flew far far up and then down and landed in the middle of the sea. Perú then hid the bird in his hand while he pretended to pick up a stone that was the same colour. He threw the bird, and it

169

flew far far up and up until it passed the middle of the sea and disappeared over the horizon.

The king stood open-mouthed, then he became annoyed, then furious. By the time he turned to thrash Perú, the man had already scarpered and was some distance down the road. The king snorted in fury and went after him. The chase continued until he had closed the distance considerably, and Perú was nearly dead with fatigue with his tongue lolling out of his mouth. Suddenly, Perú stopped, pulled down his trousers and bent over with his bum in the air. The king stopped behind him warily and said, "What do you think you're doing, Perú?"

"Quick, Your Majesty, go to your house. Beware of that stone I threw. It has a lot of magic. It's going around the world, and it will land right here. If it doesn't fall precisely in the eye of my bum, we're all going to die. That's why I'm standing in this position."

"Is that true, Perú?"

"Absolutely, Your Majesty. And when I poop the stone here the sound of a tremendous explosion will carry all the way to your house, and then you will know that we won't die."

So the king ran with all speed to his house and sat and listened. Meanwhile, Perurimá got a huge keg of gunpowder and took it to the border of the kingdom and set it off. When the king heard the blast, he said, "There. Perurimá has saved us all from a horrible fate."

Later, Perú arrived at the king's house, where he found a great party in progress, with dancing and hilarity and a generous flow of *aguardiente*.

By the time everyone was well drunk, Perú had won over the king's youngest daughter with sweet talk, and he mounted the king's own horse, lifted the princess up behind him, and galloped off down the road.

(*Aventuras*)

K18.3. Throwing contest: bird substituted for stone. The ogre throws a stone; the hero a bird which flies out of sight.

The sacristan discovered that Perurimá had sex with a nun and told him he had committed a sin and had to go to confession. Perú confessed to a priest.

"Holy God, my son, you have committed a mortal sin, and your soul is condemned to hell."

"Why is that, Padre?"

"Because you did it with a sister of God."

"But it was only through ignorance. Can you pardon me?"

"No, I'm sorry."

"So what can I do? I'm ignorant in this matter."

"You'll have to go to the bishop."

Perú confessed his sin to the bishop.

"Holy God, my son, you have committed a mortal sin, and your soul is condemned to hell."

"Why is that, Your Excellency?"

"Your soul is lost because you fornicated with a sister of God."

"Can you pardon me?"

"No. Only the Pope can do that."

"But I'm a poor man. I can't afford to go to Rome."

"There is nothing I can do about it."

"Well, if you won't pardon me, and I can't go to the Pope, I'll just have to come to some sort of understanding with my brother-in-law."

(*Huellas*)

Perurimá grew up in the house of the king, among the princesses, and one day he happened to see the youngest one naked and noticed a mole next to the lip of her concha. Later he travelled around the world, but eventually came back to work in the king's house, still a young man. The king decided it was time to marry off his youngest daughter to the man who could guess on what part of her body there was a mole. Whoever guessed wrong would have his head cut off.

Many young men wanted to marry the princess, but they were afraid they might lose their heads. Perurimá was walking around with a smile on his face.

"What do you find so amusing, Perú?" asked one of his friends.

"I'm happy because I'm the only one who knows where the princess wears a mole."

"Where is it?"

"It's next to the lip of her concha. In the morning, I'm going to tell the king and marry her."

But his friend, a scrawny, malnourished mule driver, got there first and answered the question correctly. The king was astounded.

"How do you know that?" said the king.

"I am very clever, Your Majesty, and I want to marry the princess."

So the king reluctantly announced that he had found a husband for his youngest daughter. But Perú came to him and said, "Surely you're not going to marry her to that scarecrow?"

"Why not? He answered the question correctly."

"Because I'm the one who told him where her mole is located."

"So where is it?"

"Next to the lip of her concha."

"How do you know that?"

"I am very clever and want to marry your daughter."

The king went to the mule driver and said, "Perurimá tells me that he was the one who told you where the princess's mole is."

"No, Your Majesty. He's lying. I'm the one who told him."

The king came up with a test to establish who was the true winner. He announced:

"Tonight, my daughter will sleep between you two men. Whichever of you she turns to while she is asleep will marry her. I will cut off the head of the other one."

He took a large white sheet and laid it out along a corridor and put the princess in the middle and Perurimá

172

and the mule driver at opposite ends. He sat on a cushion to watch. The princess and the mule driver slept, and Perú pretended to snore. When the rooster started to crow, Perú was worried. He opened his eyes just enough to see that the princess hadn't moved or turned to one side or the other, and the king had fallen asleep. He rose quietly and went to the other side of the princess, dropped his trousers and quickly made a large defecation. He pulled up his trousers and returned to his place and pretended to sleep.

The king awoke and stood up to stretch. He looked at the sleepers just as the stench of Perú's deposit reached the dainty nose of the princess. Without waking, she turned away from the odour and toward Perú. When the king saw that, he proclaimed that Perurimá would marry the princess and the mule driver would be executed.

(*Huellas*)

Charlie Meyers and the Barewalker
Michigan, United States

The venerable Algonquin Club of Detroit (Michigan) and Windsor (Ontario), founded in 1934, is dedicated to regional history, encompassing the Great Lakes area of Michigan and southern Ontario. The membership includes distinguished professional historians and amateur enthusiasts. Presentations are "delivered by a speaker with expertise in the area of discussion", according to their current website.

I was a member in the early 1960s, when a featured speaker at one gathering was Charlie Meyers, a book seller in downtown Detroit. His mother was from one of the tribes of the Algonquian language group – "Algonquin" refers to a subgroup – and he had an intense interest in his Native American heritage, especially the practice of barewalking.

I had read folklorist Richard Dorson's 1952 book *Bloodstoppers and Bearwalkers: Folk Traditions of the Upper Peninsula* [of Michigan] and was familiar with the

173

subject. There are three theories to explain how it works. One: a person telepathically controls an animal. Two: one of the person's three souls inhabits the animal and controls it. Three: the person strips naked and physically shape-shifts into the animal. The "bare" in "barewalking" reflects that last theory. The word is often spelled "bearwalking" because the animal most frequently employed is a bear, since the purpose of the operation is usually destruction, but I know of one case in which a woman took on the form of a wolf in order to rob traps.

Charlie told us he had identified six barewalkers in the Michigan-Ontario region, and he approached one of them, an old woman living in a cabin in the woods near the town of Saint Ignace in the Upper Peninsula of Michigan, to ask her to initiate him into the practice. But first he tested her to see if she was genuine.

He knocked on her door, she answered, he explained his mission, she invited him in. He asked her if she could barewalk anything. Yes. The wind? Yes. Show me. Where do you want it? Here. Charlie made a one-cubic-foot shape in front of him with his hands. There were no doors or windows open. Immediately, he could feel the wind in that location but not elsewhere in the cabin. Hand in the box – wind. Hand out of the box – no wind.

They went into Saint Ignace at the northern end of the Mackinac Bridge, which connects the Lower and Upper Peninsulas at the meeting of Lakes Michigan and Huron. Seagulls were flying around. Charlie indicated one.

"Can you barewalk that seagull?"

"Yes. What do you want me to make it do?"

"Make it fly away from the flock in that direction." He pointed.

As soon as he finished saying that, the gull changed direction. Charlie requested several manoeuvres, and the gull obeyed instantly.

"What else can you make it do?"

"I can make it shit."

"Do it."

The bird did, and again and again on command.

174

Charlie spied a dog and a postman.

"Can you make that dog chase the postman?"

It did, until Charlie called it off. He was convinced. He asked the woman if she could teach him how to be a barewalker. She said he had to gather certain herbs at certain times of the year and bring them to her the following January. He did that and turned up at her cabin at the agreed time. She instructed him to make a paste of the herbs and stand outside in the snow and take his clothes off and rub the paste all over his body. He did that, and nothing happened.

"When did you last have a bath?" she asked.

"This morning, just before I drove up here."

"Oh, no," she said. "That's the problem. You have to not take a bath for at least two weeks before you use the herb paste."

And that was the end of Charlie's talk. There were no giggles from the audience. We all took it seriously.

A few years later, I tried to find Charlie independently to ask him if there was a sequel to the story, but to no avail, and again recently through the Algonquin Club, but the current members had never heard of him.

Wendy Rose, in her 1977 poem "For the White poets who would be Indian", says: "You think of us only when / your voice wants for roots, / when you have sat back on / your heels and become / primitive."

The Sacred Hoop – the culture and traditions – of the Native Americans was destroyed by European colonialism, and their religion and language were taken away, not forgetting the genocide. There is understandable resistance against even the most sympathetic and sensitive Whites intruding into what remains.

I believe that the old woman never intended to teach Charlie how to be a barewalker, because he was obviously not a full-blooded Native, and she worked out an elaborate trick in order to discourage him from trying again.

On the Scent of a Thief
China

The emperor's minister of justice had a reputation as a wise man, but no one could say exactly why.

"That man is stupid as any of us," said a peasant to his friends. "It's only because of his position that people think he's intelligent."

"Why don't you expose him?" they asked. "Then maybe the emperor will replace him with you."

"I'll do that," he said, and they all laughed.

He disguised himself as a poor monk and set off along the roads begging. Most people gave him at least something, and even his father, who failed to recognize him, put a coin in his hand. Emboldened by this, he felt he was ready to expose the minister as a fool. He went to the ferry that was used exclusively by wealthy merchants to transport their valuable goods across the river. It was guarded by soldiers, who kept the general public away.

"You are not allowed here," they told the peasant as he started to board. "There is a lot of money on the ferry, and if we're not careful any thief could take advantage."

He pretended that he didn't hear and continued on to the ferry.

"Ah, leave him alone," said one of the soldiers. "He's only a poor monk. What harm can he do?"

The merchants were suspicious, and with good reason. The ferry had no sooner left the dock when the peasant began berating them.

"You suck the blood of the poor and grow fat on it. Repent, and perhaps you will break the onerous cycle of reincarnation."

"What can we do? We are only merchants."

"Recite the hundred names of Buddha."

They did so, but the peasant was not satisfied.

"Do you not feel the presence of Death? Repeat the hundred names of the Buddha with more enthusiasm."

They repeated the hundred names with such fervour that they hypnotized one another and fell into a trance.

176

The peasant stole everything he could carry and marched off the boat as soon as it reached the other bank. When the atrocity was reported to the minister, he was astonished.

"A monk robbed all the merchants on the ferry?"

"Yes. It's a divine punishment. We even saw how he flew in the air."

When the people heard about the affair, they said, "Our minister of justice isn't as astute as we thought. If a humble monk can rob with impunity, what might a real bandit be capable of?"

The peasant disguised himself as a woman. He was young enough to have almost no facial hair, and his eyes were soft and melancholy. Also, one of the things he had stolen on the ferry was a rare perfume that intoxicated all who smelled it.

"What a beautiful woman," said those he passed in the street when the scent trailing behind him bewitched their noses. "How is it that we've never seen her before?"

Even the minister of justice fell in love with her and proposed marriage.

"I can't accept," the peasant said. "My father was a dealer in pearls. He died far across the seas. A fisherman sent me his ashes, and I can't marry until I have buried them where he requested."

"Why don't you do that?"

"Because the place is on the other side of the river, and I'm afraid I might meet with that thief."

The minister ordered the army to guard the fair maiden.

"You will pay with your lives if anything happens to her," he warned the soldiers.

As soon as he boarded the ferry, the peasant began to flirt with the soldiers. They fought with one another until every one of them had fallen into the river. Then he collected all the valuables left behind and escaped when the boat reached the other bank.

"That thief again," said the minister when he found out. "He's a demon from hell. And to think I was about to marry her ... him."

Then he remembered her enchanting perfume and came up with a plan. He went to one of the merchants who had been robbed on the ferry, the merchant whose perfume the peasant had stolen.

"I'll give you all the perfume I have, if it will help you catch that thief," he told the minister.

"That won't be necessary. I only need a small amount."

He hired a particularly unattractive woman and told her to apply the perfume and walk through hotel lobbies and taverns, while he and two policemen in plain clothes observed the results. She did this night after night until finally she walked through a certain tavern. As usual, the men's heads turned as soon as she passed and the scent entered their nostrils. But sitting at one table was a man who continued talking to his companions – or to the sides of their heads – and who was obviously immune to the perfume.

"Seize that man," the minister ordered the policemen. "That's the thief who has been causing me so much headache."

"I'm an honest man," the peasant protested. "What proof do you have that I'm a thief?"

"Every man who smells that perfume turns to look, except you. And that is because you are accustomed to it, because you wore it when you were disguised as a woman."

The Pardoner's Tale
The Canterbury Tales – Chaucer
Britain

Early one morning three rogues were drinking in a tavern, when they heard the tolling of a bell in the street that indicated a funeral procession.

"Boy," they called to the waiter. "Go see who's being buried."

"I don't have to ask, sir. I know it's an old friend of yours. Just two hours before you arrived, he was sitting on

178

a bench when a shady thief called Death stuck a spear into his heart and killed him. He's killed at least a thousand around here recently. My mother told me you have to be on guard. You never know when you might run into him."

"There are three of us and only one of him," said one of the rogues. "If you two are with me, we'll search the high roads and the by-roads and kill this Death who has killed so many."

The other two, drunk and furious, swore loyalty to one another, and they set off to find Death. They had gone less than half a mile when they met a poor old man wrapped in a cloak so only his face was visible. He greeted them kindly.

"God save ye, gentlemen."

"It looks like God has saved you too long, old man," said the most arrogant of the rogues. "Why are you still alive?"

"God only knows. Death keeps passing me by."

"Speaking of Death, that's who we're looking for. Do you know where we can find him?"

"If it's Death ye seek, I just left him under an oak tree in a grove at the top of that crooked lane. And God save ye who saved mankind."

The rogues ran up the lane into the grove, where they found eight bushels of gold florins under the oak, and they forgot all about their search for Death.

"Look what fortune has given us," said the most villainous of the three. "We'll take it to one of our houses and divide it. But we can't move it in broad daylight. People will think we stole it. We'll wait till dark. Let's draw straws to see who goes into town to buy food and drink while the other two stay and guard the treasure."

The youngest drew the short straw, and off he went into the town. As soon as he was gone, one said to the other, "Wouldn't it be better to divide this gold into two parts instead of three? What do you say?"

"What would we tell the young fellow?"

"We tell him nothing. It's two against one. When he comes back, you start a bit of horseplay with him, and when you have him down, I'll stab him in the side, and you do the same."

The other rogue agreed. Meanwhile, the youngest rogue was thinking it would be better not to have to divide the treasure at all. He went to a chemist and said, "I'm plagued with rats, and a polecat has been killing my chickens. Can you sell me some poison that will solve my problem?"

The chemist said, "I have a concoction that will kill any creature that eats or drinks a drop of it in less time than it takes to walk a mile."

The young man bought the poison and went to another shop, where he bought food and three bottles of wine. He put the poison into two bottles, keeping one safe for later, after he had moved all the gold to his house.

As planned, the two rogues killed the young one as soon as he returned with the provisions, and then they sat down to have a drink before disposing of the body. As luck would have it, they chose the poisoned bottles.

This story is also found in French, Indian, Jewish, Korean and Chinese tradition.

K1685. The treasure-finders who murder one another. Two (three) men find a treasure. One of them secretly puts poison in the other's wine, but the other kills him, drinks the wine and dies.

The Bossy Woman
Zamora, Spain

There was a woman who was so bossy she killed all four of her husbands because they wouldn't obey her orders. A man who lived in the town was in love with her. His friends said, "Are you crazy? No one can put up with that woman."

"She doesn't scare me," he said. "I'm going to marry her, and you'll see that she won't get the better of me."

His friends bet him that she would win.

They got married. She owned two fine fat young bulls. The man exchanged them for two skinny old bulls without telling her. Then he came into the house and said, "Since it's our first day as a married couple, let's go out and inspect our property." So they set off on the burra. It was a moonlit night. They dismounted and continued on foot. When they went to look for the burra later, she had disappeared.

"I'm going to kill that burra when I find her," he said.

They eventually found her near the house. He went into the house and got a shotgun and shot the burra twice in the head and killed her.

"What have you done?" the woman said.

"What I always do to someone who goes against me."

The woman was frightened and said, "You have done well, my husband. You have done very well." And to herself, she said, "He's a killer. I'd better not argue with him. Live and learn."

Then he showed her the two old bulls he had substituted for her fine young ones. "How do you like them?" he asked her.

"Good, very good. They look fine and fat to me."

"They're not fine and fat," he said. "They're old and skinny. The ones I exchanged for these were fine and fat."

"Yes, yes. Whatever you say."

They went into the house and he said, "Woman, bring me the bandurria [mandolin] that I bought at the market today."

She brought him the bandurria, and he began to play and sing:

> Woman, I come from the fair.
> I bought this bandurria there.
> The burra she fled,
> And now she is dead.
> Remember, woman – take care.

He collected his wager from his friends, and the man and the woman lived ... Well, at least they both lived.

181

(Loosely translated and retold from "La mujer mandona", Espinosa, *Cuentos Populares Españoles*.)

Students at a secondary school in Spain were given a literary variant of this folk tale and asked for their reactions. A group of them composed their own version. A bossy man had three wives. He threatened them with violence if they didn't do as he ordered. The women decided to play a trick on him. They prepared the supper and then disguised themselves as men. When the husband came home, he found three supposed men, who told him they had seen the women riding off with three men on horseback. He got angry and then he got drunk, and when he passed out the women tied him to a table. When he woke up, the women took off their disguises and told him they would untie him if he promised to share the household tasks with them and respect them and not be so bossy. Then they took the bandurria and sang:

> From the fiesta we came,
> Dressed as three men for a game.
> Remember, our spouse,
> That this is our house,
> Where all are treated the same.

On a similar theme, John Malcolm relates this story in his *Sketches of Persia*.

Sâdik Beg married a woman of fearsome reputation. On their wedding night, he decapitated her cat in front of her and threw the remains out the window, and she became kind and submissive ever after. His friend, Merdek, who was unhappily married, asked him for the secret of his success, and Sâdik told him what he had done. Merdek went home and decapitated his wife's cat in front of her, not suspecting that she had heard the story of Sâdik and his wife from the other women. As he bent down to throw the remains out the window, his wife clouted him in the head and continued to beat him, saying, "You should have killed the cat on our wedding night."

182

The Perfect Wife
Widespread

A man ran into an old friend he hadn't seen in many years. As they exchanged news, he said, "By the way, I got married since the last time I saw you."

"Oh, really? How often do you beat your wife?"

The man was astounded.

"Beat her? Why should I beat her? She's a perfect wife – kind, loving, sweet, patient, efficient."

"Take my advice. I've been married longer than you have, and I know how to handle women. If you don't beat them regularly they can get out of hand. They think they're the boss. I beat my wife at least once a week, and I'm happily married."

"But I have no reason to beat her. She never does anything wrong."

"Then make an excuse. For example, buy some fish, take it home, tell your wife you have important guests coming for dinner, and then leave without telling her how you want it cooked. When you come home, whatever way she's cooked it, tell her it's not how you wanted it. Then you have an excuse to beat her."

The man took the advice, neglecting to ask if the friend's wife was as happily married as the friend. He bought a big fish, took it home, told his wife that important people were coming to dinner, and left without telling her how to cook it. She thought for a moment and came up with a solution. She boiled part of the fish, baked part of it and fried the rest.

Just as she heard her husband at the door, a chicken came into the kitchen from the back garden and deposited a squirt of pooh on the floor. With no time to clean it up, she placed a pot over the indiscretion so no one would step in it. Instead of leaving his walking stick at the front door as usual, the husband carried it into the kitchen.

"Is the fish ready to be served?" he asked brusquely.

She showed him the piece of fish in the frying pan.

"That's not how I wanted it cooked," he said, raising the stick above his head.

She lifted the lid off the pot of the boiled portion.

"That's not how I wanted it cooked," he said, lowering the stick halfway.

She opened the oven to show him the baked portion.

"Shit," he said, lowering the stick all the way.

She lifted the pot off the chicken pooh.

He dropped the stick and embraced her, saying, to her confusion, "I'll never listen to anyone's advice again. You're the perfect wife."

J1545.3. Fault-finding husband nonplussed. The wife has cooked so many dishes that when he complains, she can always supply another. Finally he says, "I had rather eat dung." She produces some.

"The best advice is this: don't take anyone's advice."
Mark Twain

The Postman from Purgatory
Erro, Navarre, Basque Country

A woman whose husband had died married again, but she could never stop thinking about her first husband. This was well known to everyone in the town. One day a man knocked on her door, and when she asked who it was he answered, "I'm the Postman from Purgatory."

"Oh," she said. "My first husband is dead and I haven't heard anything from him yet."

"In fact," said the Postman from Purgatory, "the message I have is from your late husband, and he says that he needs one more Mass said for him so he can go to heaven, but he doesn't have the money to pay for the Mass."

The woman gave him all the money she had in the house. When her current husband arrived home, she said with satisfaction, "The Postman from Purgatory was here, and he told me that my late husband needed one more

184

Mass to get into heaven, so I gave him all our money to open the Pearly Gates."

The husband was angry with his wife, but he wasted no time abusing her for her foolishness. He quickly jumped on his horse and set off down the road. He encountered a traveller, who, unbeknownst to the husband, was the very man he was seeking, and asked him if he had seen the Postman from Purgatory.

"Yes," said the man. "He went up that road." He pointed to a mountain track inaccessible by horseback.

The husband dismounted, leaving his horse in the care of the Postman, and walked a distance along the indicated path without encountering anyone. He returned to where he had left his horse to find both horse and traveller gone. When he finally arrived home on foot, his wife asked him what had become of the horse. He told her that he had overtaken the Postman from Purgatory and given him the horse, in order to speed him on his way to get the Mass said so that her late husband would not have to spend any more time suffering the fires of Purgatory than was necessary.

Pedro uses this scam in the play *Pedro de Urdemalas* by Cervantes, 1615. His Chilean descendant, Pedro Urdemales, played a similar trick as Saint Peter's postman.

K346.1. Thief guards his pursuer's horse while the latter follows a false trail. Steals the horse.

According to Barbara Lutz in *The Brontë Cabinet*, Victorians buried letters to the deceased in postmen's coffins in the belief that they would deliver them.

The Three Riddles of the King Who Went Mad
Spain

The priest of San Babilés was renowned for his wisdom and learning – a fountain of knowledge, according to his parishioners – but the goatherd Marcos did not participate in the consensus. He scandalized his neighbours by saying, "The priest doesn't even know half

185

of the Mass." The priest had a lower opinion of Marcos: "He doesn't even know the Latin word for 'goat'."

The king was such an avid student of learning that he had nearly lost his senses, for which he was known as the King Who Went Mad. He heard about this paragon of erudition in San Babilés and went to visit him. When he arrived at the priest's house, he was surprised that the priest did not come out to greet him. The priest excused his dereliction of social duty by explaining that the soup had just been set on the table, and he didn't want it to get cold.

The king and the priest sat side by side in the parlour. The king found the priest's chubby cheeks off-putting, but he said to himself, "I shouldn't judge on appearances. If he prefers hot soup to greeting the king, he must be a stoic philosopher, and his fat cheeks could come from the satisfaction of possessing vast knowledge." But after fifteen minutes of questions and answers it became clear that the priest was nothing more than a vain, ignorant, boasting know-it-all and a glutton.

"I have to give him a lesson in humility," the king thought. "Instead of eating to live and living to serve God, he lives to eat and serves only himself."

"Señor Priest," he said, "I can see that your reputation for sagacity is well merited, but to convince myself of that I'm going to ask you three little questions, which I'm sure you will answer satisfactorily without taxing your brain. You will have one month to give me your response."

"Your Majesty may ask whatever you like," said the priest, striking a pose. "I'm ready any time."

"Very good. I've been looking for someone astute enough to answer these questions. First, how much am I worth? Second, how much time will it take me to go around the world? Third, in what way am I mistaken in what I'm thinking? A wise man such as yourself should be able to answer off the top of your head, but there's no hurry. I'll expect you at my palace a month from today with your reply. If you answer correctly, I'll make you the *archipámpano* of Seville. If you fail, you will be led through the streets mounted on a burro and given six lashes at every corner."

(The priest didn't know that *archipámpano* was a fictitious post of eminence that the king made up on the spot.)

"But, but," the priest sputtered.

The King Who Went Mad put on a face like a mad dog and said, "No arguments. Your king has spoken."

The weeks passed, and the priest had no idea how to solve the riddles. Unwilling to admit his ignorance, he indirectly sought the advice of his parishioners:

"Hey, you, clodhopper, what would you say if the king asked you ...?"

They didn't know either, and, pretending that he had the answer himself, he abused them for their ignorance. As his appointment with the king approached, he became more and more emaciated. He barely ate or slept, pondering the three questions and picturing himself on a burro and being whipped through the streets.

Meanwhile, Marcos the goatherd grew fatter and fatter. He knew about the questions and was swollen with satisfaction at the suffering of the priest, who had so often insulted him for not knowing the Latin word for "goat".

The day before the priest was due to visit the palace, Marcos organized a "chance" encounter with him and asked him why he looked so depressed.

"What's it to you?" snapped the priest.

"I thought I might be of some help."

"How could you help? You're just an animal who doesn't even know Latin grammar."

"Look, Señor Priest, let's not pretend that I don't know you're in for a flogging tomorrow if you don't have the answers to the king's questions. I can help you if you trust me. I may not know Latin grammar, but I do know brown grammar."

("Brown grammar" is the instinctive and clever logic of the uneducated brown-clothed peasants.)

"What? Do you know how much the king is worth, how long it will take him to go around the world, and what is the mistake in what he's thinking?"

"Never mind that for now. At dawn tomorrow, we will change clothes. I will go dressed as a priest to the palace in your place, while you wear my goatherd clothes and stay here to look after the goats."

The desperate priest had no choice but to agree to the plan. Since he had slimmed considerably over the month, and Marcos had grown fat, the clothes they exchanged fitted perfectly.

Marcos arrived at the palace and introduced himself as the priest, and he was presented as such when he was led into the presence of the king.

"Señor Priest, you are prepared to answer my three questions?"

"I am, Your Majesty."

"And you know the penalty for failure?"

"Yes, Your Majesty."

"So, then. The first question: how much am I worth?"

"Twenty-nine pieces of silver."

"How dare you!" said the King Who Went Mad, with a ferocious look on his face.

"Jesus Christ was valued at thirty pieces of silver, and I'm sure Your Majesty would not pretend to be worth as much as Christ."

"I'll accept that answer. Now the second question: how long will it take me to go around the world?"

"If Your Majesty is mounted on the sun, it will take twenty-four hours."

"Well answered," said the king, who, like his courtiers, had only the vaguest knowledge of astronomy. They all applauded this response, as they had the first, once the king had accepted it.

"The third question – and will it win you the post of *archipámpano* of Seville, or ...?" the king said tantalizingly. "In what way am I mistaken in what I'm thinking?"

"You think I'm the priest of San Babilés."

"We have a flogging!" shouted the king, mad with satisfaction.

"We have a flogging!" shouted the courtiers gleefully.

"No, señor," said Marcos. "There will be no flogging. Do you not think that I am the priest of San Babilés?"

"Yes, but you have not pointed out the error in my thinking."

"I'm not the priest. I'm the goatherd."

"Prove it."

Just at that moment, in rushed the mayor of San Babilés.

"Your Majesty, a terrible thing has happened in San Babilés. The goatherd Marcos has disappeared, and the priest has gone crazy and is dressed in the goatherd's clothes and is tending the goats in his place."

It soon became clear that it was the goatherd who had answered the king's questions perfectly. The King Who Went Mad appointed Marcos to the newly established post of *archipámpano* of Seville with a salary of ten thousand *reales* a year – a very comfortable living – and he ordered the priest to keep wearing the goatherd's clothes and tend the goats for a month.

(Based on "Gramática Parda" in *Cuentos Populares* by Antonio de Trueba.)

H561.2. King and abbot. King propounds three riddles to abbot to answer on pain of death. Herdsman disguises as abbot and answers questions.

H524.1. "What am I thinking?" "That I am the priest." So answers youth masking as priest.

Q473.5.2. Riding backwards on donkey as punishment.

A similar story appears in the 16th-century *Tarlton's Newes out of Purgatorie*, and a more distant relative is in the 14th-century Gesta Romanorum. A popular version called "King John and the Abbot of Canterbury" is found in Percy's *Reliques*, 1765. Here the king propounds the riddles to the abbot:

"And first," quo' the king, "when I'm in this stead,
With my crowne of golde so faire on my head,

189

Among all my liege-men so noble of birthe,
Thou must tell me to one penny what I am worthe.

"Secondlye, tell me, without any doubt,
How soone I may ride the whole world about.
And at the third question thou must not shrink,
But tell me here truly what I do think."

A 17th-century version carries the moral tag:

"Unlearned men hard matters out can find,
When learned bishops princes eyes do blind."

Saints and Sieges
Ukraine and Russia

The nucleus of modern Russia was an enclave of
Eastern Slavs dominated by a ninth-century incursion of
Danish Vikings called the Rus (approximate
pronunciation: "roos") established by Rurik and centred
on Novgorod. On his deathbed in 879, Rurik entrusted the
care of his young son, Igor, to his kinsman, Oleg, who he
named as his successor. Oleg moved the capital of the
principality to Kiev, for which the people became known
as the Kievan Rus.

Death of Oleg

According to the *Primary Chronicle*, a 12th-century
compendium of history and legend, Oleg asked his
magicians how he would die. They said his death would
come through his stallion. So Oleg commanded that the
horse be taken away and properly looked after. Many
years later he asked what had become of the horse. He was
told that it was dead. He went to the place where it had
died, looked at the skeletal remains and laughed: "The
magicians lied. The horse is dead but I'm still alive." He

kicked the horse's skull in derision. A poisonous snake slithered out of the skull and bit him, and he died.

Death of Igor

The following year, 913, Igor became prince. He extended the rule of the Kievan Rus to dominate a loose federation of tribes and principalities that alternately quarrelled and allied with each other. Igor had to repeatedly subdue his nearest neighbour to the west, Dereva, a heavily forested principality where a major industry was fur-trapping. The *Primary Chronicle* states that the Derevlians (the name means "forest dwellers") "existed in bestial fashion, and lived like cattle. They killed one another, ate every impure thing, and there was no marriage between them, but instead they seized upon maidens by capture." The Rus mockingly referred to them as "tree people", the equivalent of "hillbillies".

The Derevlians had been dragging their feet on paying a tribute that had been levied by Oleg and later doubled by Igor. In 945, Igor went with an army and collected it after quickly defeating them. On his way back to Kiev, the idea occurred to him that he should have doubled the tribute again. Overconfident following his easy victory, he turned back to their capital, Iskorosten (modern Korosten), about 80 miles (130km) northwest of Kiev, with only a small retinue and made his demand. Encouraged by their prince, Mal, "to rise and slay the wolf who was bent on devouring their whole flock," the Derevlians killed him. The tenth-century Byzantine chronicler Leo the Deacon reported that years later, when Igor's son, Svyatoslav I "the Brave", threatened the Romans toward the end of his short but active life – he died at 30 – they reminded him of "the wretched fate" of his father: "tied to tree trunks, and torn in two".

Olga's Revenge

Mal sent a delegation of 20 prominent citizens to Kiev to propose marriage to Igor's widow, Olga (890-969). The Derevlians arrived in a boat and sent a message informing Olga of the purpose of their visit. She understood that Mal's intention was to annex Kiev by controlling her and the then three-year-old Svyatoslav, in whose interests she was acting as regent. She told them to spend the night in their boat, and her people would show their respect by carrying them in the boat to her palace in the morning, where she could greet them formally. Then she had a deep ditch dug in the courtyard of her palace. When the delegation arrived in the morning, they were tipped into the ditch with the boat on top of them. The ditch was filled in, burying them alive.

The *Primary Chronicle* reports: "Olga then sent messages to the Derevlians to the effect that, if they really required her presence, they should send after her their distinguished men, so that she might go to their Prince with due honour, for otherwise her people in Kiev would not let her go." When "the best men who governed the land of Dereva" arrived, Olga suggested they refresh themselves in the bathhouse before she received them. Once the visitors were all inside, the Kievans closed and locked the doors and set fire to the building.

Then she sent a message to Dereva to say that she was on her way to Iskorosten, "so prepare great quantities of mead in the city where you killed my husband, that I may weep over his grave and hold a funeral feast for him." They did so. When she arrived with a small escort, she told her people to stay sober and serve the drink to the Derevlians. The funeral feast was well under way before the Derevlians thought to inquire as to the whereabouts of the nobles they had sent to Kiev to accompany her. She assured them that they were following with her husband's bodyguard. When the Derevlians were drunk, she ordered her people to kill them. They massacred five thousand.

Olga returned to Kiev and assembled an army for a full-scale invasion of Dereva. She succeeded in subduing the countryside and smaller cities and towns, but Iskorosten was too well defended, and she laid siege to it. After a year, she sent a message: "Why do you persist in holding out? All your cities have surrendered to me and submitted to tribute, so that the inhabitants now cultivate their fields and their lands in peace." They replied that they would gladly submit to tribute, but they were afraid of her vengeance. She said she had enough revenge, and, since they were now impoverished by the siege, she would return to Kiev on receiving a mere token tribute: three sparrows and three pigeons from each household. The Derevlians gladly complied with the generous offer and returned to the city rejoicing.

Olga instructed her soldiers to attach a piece of tinder enclosed in cloth to the birds' feet. After dark, they lit the tinder and loosed the birds, which predictably flew to their nests in the eaves of the houses and barns. The whole city was instantly engulfed in flame. Many of those who weren't killed in the fire were slaughtered as they tried to escape. Olga took some as slaves and left just enough of the elders to pay tribute. She then ranged through Dereva establishing trading posts and appointing local tax collectors, so that never again would the Kievan Rus prince have to risk his life gathering tribute personally.

Olga would certainly have been familiar with stories of earlier occasions, perhaps legendary, when fire-bearing birds were used to destroy a city under siege. One of many examples was when a Dane named Fridleif used the same trick to take Dublin at an unspecified date, as reported by the 13-14th-century Danish historian Saxo Grammaticus. Probably the best known is the burning of Cirencester by the Saxons in 552 (ST motif K2351.1). See chapter "The Birds of Cirencester". During the Second World War, the United States developed a similar scheme for dropping Bat Bombs on Japan, but it was abandoned in favour of the atomic bomb. There is a curious current rumour or urban legend that Korosten has recently filed a lawsuit against

Kiev demanding compensation for Olga's destruction of the city.

Kiev Under Siege

Olga and Igor's son, Svyatoslav, had been busy expanding the Kievan Rus sphere of domination and was away from Kiev when the Pechenegs invaded the Rus heartland and laid siege to Kiev at the instigation of the Byzantines, who were worried about the increasing power of the Rus. Olga was in the city with her grandsons, including Vladimir, who became Grand Prince after Svyatoslav's death. The city, which is on the Dnieper River and is now divided by it, was so tightly encircled that a small band of Rus warriors camped on the other side of the river was unable to help, nor could anyone escape from the city. The citizens were suffering from hunger and thirst and were ready to surrender. A young man who was fluent in the Pecheneg language volunteered to try to cross the river to inform the warriors of the dire situation.

He sneaked out of the city with a bridle in his hand and ran among the Pechenegs asking if anyone had seen a loose horse. They assumed he was one of them and didn't realize what he was up to until he threw off his clothes and dived into the river and began to swim across it. They shot at him, but he was picked up uninjured by the Rus warriors in a boat. When he told them that unless help arrived by the following day the city would surrender, the leader, Pretich, came up with a bold plan.

In the morning before dawn they set off across the river blowing their trumpets, and the people in the city shouted with jubilation, assuming that Svyatoslav had arrived with his army. The Pecheneg soldiers assumed the same thing and started to scatter. Olga and her grandsons came out and boarded the boats. The Pecheneg leader saw this and approached Pretich and asked if he was Prince Svyatoslav. Pretich told him that he was the leader of the vanguard, and that Svyatoslav and his army were close behind him, so the Pecheneg leader formally lifted the siege.

194

Olga and Vladimir Convert to Christianity

Perhaps sensing the way the political wind was blowing, Olga decided to become a Christian in 957. She asked Emperor Constantine VII (905-959) to be her godfather, ostensibly for the prestige, but also for another good reason. She knew he was in love with her and wanted to marry her. She wasn't interested, but it would not have been politically expedient to refuse his offer. She deflected his hints by saying that she would have to be baptized first. After the ceremony, he formally proposed. She pointed out that he was now her father in God, and the Christian Law did not permit a father to marry his daughter. Constantine admired her cleverness and took the rejection gracefully.

Olga was declared a saint of the Russian Orthodox Church in 1547 with the title of *isapóstolos*, which means "equal to the apostles", one of only a handful of saints so honoured.

Svyatoslav rebuffed Olga's urgings to become Christian, but his son Vladimir the Great (c. 958-1015), a dedicated pagan early in life, investigated various religions before eventually choosing Eastern Orthodox Christianity and making it the state religion. He is recognized as a saint in Eastern Orthodoxy and other faiths. Two of his sons were Saint Boris and Saint Gleb.

One More Siege

Vladimir founded the city of Belgorod in 991. The Rus were in continual conflict with the Pechenegs, and in 997 he went to Novgorod to recruit reinforcements to help him settle the problem. The Pechenegs discovered his absence and laid siege to Belgorod. The citizens were unprepared and had few provisions, and they were soon on the brink of starvation. They held a council and decided to surrender. Even though some of them might be killed, they felt it was better than all starving to death. An old man had a better idea.

He told them to dig two pits for two tubs, gather oats, wheat and bran to make a porridge in one tub and pour diluted honey in the other. When this was done, he told them to send ten messengers as goodwill hostages to the Pechenegs and invite ten of them to enter the city to see what was happening.

When the Pechenegs arrived, they were told that even if they kept up the siege for ten years they could never take Belgorod, because the people would never run out of food. As proof, the citizens led the Pechenegs to the tubs where the porridge and honey seemed to be delivered ready-to-eat directly from the earth. They ate some themselves to show it was safe and gave the visitors a taste. The Pechenegs were amazed. They took bowls of the food back to their leaders, who saw the futility of the siege and went home.

Gurdafrid Fights Sohrab
Greater Iran
from the tenth-century Persian epic, the *Shahnameh*

Sohrab, son of the major hero of the *Shahnameh*, Rostam, was duped into leading an invasion into Iran, where Rostam was champion and chief defender. He arrived with his army at the White Castle, the main Iranian fortress, where Hujir was in charge. Hujir came out to challenge Sohrab in single combat and was quickly defeated and taken captive.

When Hujir's warrior daughter, Gurdafrid, saw that, she donned her armour, tucked her hair under her helmet, mounted her warhorse, and sallied forth from the castle, roaring a challenge to the champions of the invaders to meet her in single combat. She looked formidable, and none of the champions volunteered. But Sohrab stepped forward and said, "I will accept your challenge, and a second prize will fall into my hands."

He mounted his horse and approached Gurdafrid, but her arrows fell on him like hail, and he had to cover his head with his shield. He charged, and she set her lance and nearly unseated him. He managed to grab her horse's reins and threw her to the ground, but she drew her sword to fend him off and mounted her horse and galloped toward the castle. He caught up with her and threw her down again, and this time tore off her helmet so he could see who his opponent was. Amazed to find it was a woman, he said, "If all the Iranian women are like you, no one can take the land."

He started to tie her up to take her prisoner, but she said, "Do you think it's a good idea to allow your soldiers see that you were nearly brought down by a woman? To save you embarrassment, I suggest we agree a truce. I'll surrender the castle. You come in with me now and take possession."

"That's a wise decision," he said, "because I'd be able to capture it with little effort."

She led him to the castle, and when the gate was opened for her, she slipped in and quickly shut it in Sohrab's face and climbed to the battlement to mock him.

"You should go back where you came from, because if a woman can beat you, you'd be no match for Rostam when he finds out that a band of robbers have entered his territory."

Sohrab rode off in search of softer targets.

María Pérez the Manly Fights the Battler
Spain

When Alfonso VI, King of Castile and León, died in 1109, his daughter, Urraca, widow of Raimundo, inherited the throne. Her and Raimundo's son was Alfonso VII (1105-1157), who was later named Emperor of All Spain. She married Alfonso I (1074-1134), King of Aragón, a bully nicknamed "the Battler", only to prevent him taking her kingdom by force, but divorced him in 1113 because

197

of his violence and cruelty. When she died in 1126, her son became king as Alfonso VII. The hardened and experienced Battler immediately issued a challenge to his young stepson: "I can beat anyone from your kingdom in single combat. Name your champion."

Three of the most renowned warriors of Castile and León were Álvar, Gómez and María Pérez. Alfonso VII nominated Álvar, who arrived in full public view at the selected venue in neutral territory on the day before the contest. María sneaked into the camp after dark, following the plan hatched by Alfonso and Álvar: María would fight the Battler dressed in Álvar's armour.

In the morning, Alfonso of Aragón and his opponent, faces obscured by helmets, broke several lances against each other on horseback, then proceeded to swordplay on foot. The spectators noticed that the warrior they took to be Álvar Pérez seemed to have changed his fighting style. He was more agile than usual, and he danced around the Battler giving him no rest. By late morning, the Aragón king had tired, and at midday the Castilian champion managed to disarm him and lay him on his back, sword to his throat. Alfonso yielded.

Then María dramatically removed her helmet to the astonishment of the crowd and the acute embarrassment of the Battler.

For her accomplishment, Alfonso VII conferred on her the title "la Varona – the Manly". The chastened Alfonso of Aragón was sport enough to award her the right to add the four red bars of Aragón to her coat of arms – diagonally to designate a trophy. He ceased his predatory attitude toward Castile and León, which was undoubtedly the result Alfonso VII had hoped for, and they agreed their territorial limits in the 1127 Peace of Támara. From then on, we are told, they acted like brothers or like father and son.

María's family, beginning with her son Rodrigo, substituted Varona for Pérez as their surname.

San Martín Txiki and the Basajauns
Basque Country

Long ago, only the basajauns (lords of the woods) knew how to plant, harvest and mill wheat to make flour. The basajauns kept this knowledge to themselves, but San Martín worked out a plan to steal the secret of agriculture and give it to the human race. ("Txiki", pronounced "cheeky", is Basque for "little" and is used in an affectionate sense.)

San Martín made a bet with the basajauns to see who could jump over the heaps of wheat they had harvested. The basajauns laughed at San Martín, because they knew that a mere human would be no competition for them, and they laughed at his big floppy shoes. They all jumped over the wheat easily, but when San Martín tried, he landed on top of one of the heaps, and the basajauns laughed again.

Then San Martín laughed, and he laughed last and best, but quietly, because his trick had worked. Now, the basajauns are big and slow-witted, but when they saw San Martín walking away home, with his big, floppy shoes full of grains of their wheat, they realized that they had been tricked. When they stopped laughing, San Martín began to run for his life, and it's a good thing that he did.

He was already a kilometre away when one of the basajauns threw a hatchet. The lords of the woods may be slow, but they are strong. San Martín saw the hatchet coming, and he ducked behind a chestnut tree just in time. The hatchet struck the tree and split it in half.

San Martín now had the seeds, but he didn't know the right time of the year to sow them. Fortunately, a man was passing by the cave of one of the basajauns, and he heard him singing:

> If the humans knew this song
> They'd be well informed.
> When the leaf is in the bud
> Then you sow the corn.
> When the leaf falls off the trees

Then you sow the wheat.
When San Lorenzo's feast comes round
Sow the turnip in the ground.

The man told San Martín what he heard, and San Martín told all the humans, and that is how cultivation spread through the world. (The Feast of San Lorenzo is 10 August.)

San Martín wanted to know how to make a saw, so humans could cut down trees as the basajauns did and make mills to grind the wheat to make flour. The basajauns wouldn't tell, because they wanted to keep all their secrets to themselves. So San Martín sent a man to the basajauns to tell them that he had discovered the secret of making a saw.

"So he has seen the leaves of the chestnut tree, has he?" a basajaun said.

That is how San Martín learned to use the chestnut leaf as a model for making a saw blade, and humans were able to cut down trees and build flour mills. But there was a problem. The axles of the mills kept wearing out, and a lot of time was wasted in replacing them. So San Martín sent a man to tell the basajauns that he had learned how to keep the axles from wearing out.

"So he's learned to polish the axles smooth, has he?" a basajaun said.

[Variant: "So he's learned to make the axles of alder-wood, has he?"]

And again, when men started to work with metals and needed to know how to weld pieces of iron together, San Martín sent a man to tell the basajauns that he had learned how to weld.

"So he knows how to sprinkle the iron with clayey water, does he?" was the response.

Perhaps it was because the basajauns admired the humans for their great cleverness that they used to give the shepherds warning of a coming storm by whistling.

A541. Culture hero teaches arts and crafts.

Turning the Plaice
Rome

Aurelius Alexander Severus was Roman emperor from AD 222, when his cousin the emperor was conveniently assassinated, to 235, when he was assassinated. His family name suited him. He was severe, strict, harsh, serious, though he could also be just when occasion demanded.

He ordained a law for no apparent reason other than to celebrate his realm's prosperity: you could only eat the white side of a plaice; anyone who turned it over to eat the black side would be put to death. In mitigation, the condemned person was allowed to ask three favours of the emperor, which would be granted with the stipulation that the favours could not include a reprieve from execution.

One day, an earl and his son came to speak with the emperor. They were given dinner, and the earl was served with a plaice. Ignorant of Alexander's capricious law, he ate the white side and turned the fish over and ate the black side. The crime was reported to the emperor, who condemned him to death. The earl's son went to the emperor and begged to be executed instead of his father.

"As long as one of you dies, that will please me," said Alexander.

"I ask the three favours that are permitted by your law," said the son.

"That is allowed. What is the first favour that you ask?"

"That I marry your daughter."

Alexander wasn't happy about this, but he reasoned that the young man would soon be dead anyway, so he granted it.

"The second favour?"

"That you give me all your treasure."

Granted for the same reason.

"And the third?"

"That all those who saw my father eat the black side of the plaice have their eyes put out."

"By my own law, I have to grant your third favour." Turning to the accusers, Alexander said, "Now, which of you witnessed the earl eat the black side of the plaice?"

They all wisely decided that they had seen nothing, and so the earl's life was saved, and his son married the princess and inherited the emperor's fortune when he died.

(From Gesta Romanorum, Chapter XLVI.)

Two Pieces of Advice and an Empanada
Spain

Within a few days of his wedding, Juan had to leave home to seek work. After two weeks' travel he landed a position as a baker, where he was provided with room and board and the promise of a thousand *reales* per year to be paid when his employment came to an end. His employer called him Juan Cavila, not because he cavilled, but the opposite: he was impetuous and didn't always think things through. The boss kept a close eye on his work and frequently had to remind him, "Juan, cavila [pay attention to the details]!" For all that, he was a good employee, and the boss liked him, so he stayed at the job for twenty years.

One day Juan said, "Sir, I think it's time to go home to my wife."

"Your wife? I didn't know you were married. Does she ever write to you?"

"No, sir. She doesn't know where I am."

"Don't you write to her?"

"No, sir. I don't know how to write."

"Well, then, it is indeed time for you to go. I owe you 20,000 reales for the twenty years you have worked here, but I worry about what might happen if I give it to you."

"What might happen?"

"You're a good worker, Juan, but you don't think of the consequences of your actions. That's why I say, 'Juan, cavila.' You could lose the money, or someone could steal it from you. So I propose this: I'll give you two pieces of

202

advice instead, as well as an empanada for you to share with your wife when you arrive home, and enough money for the journey."

Without thinking – as usual – Juan agreed.

"Now, Juan, cavila. Here are the two pieces of advice: never leave the highway for the byway and always consult your pillow before you act."

"Consult my pillow?"

"That means to sleep on it: don't do the first thing that comes to your mind. If you follow these two pieces of advice, I promise you that they will be worth more than 20,000 reales."

"I promise."

"And, Juan, cavila: don't eat the empanada until you reach home and share it with your wife."

"Yes, sir."

Juan set off and soon fell in with a group of travellers who were going in the same direction. They came to a crossroads, and the rest of them decided to take a shortcut, but Juan remembered his boss's advice and kept to the main road. Three days later, he came across the group who had taken the shortcut. They had been beaten and robbed, and they pounced on Juan and searched him from top to toe to see if he had anything worth stealing. All they found was the empanada, which by then was quite stale, so they let him go.

It was after nightfall when Juan arrived at his house. He peered through the window to see what his wife was doing. To his shock, he saw her sitting at a table opposite a handsome young man. They were eating dinner and laughing and smiling at each other. Juan ran to the shed next to the house and took out a shotgun and loaded it. He returned to the window and aimed at the chest of the man. But then he thought of the second advice his boss had given him: "Consult your pillow before you act."

"No, not this time," he said to himself. But he remembered that he had traded 10,000 reales for each piece of advice. By following the first advice he had escaped a beating, and it might have saved his life.

Probably for the first time in his life Juan Cavila cavilled and consulted his pillow. He bedded down for the night in the shed.

At sunrise he left the shotgun in the shed and knocked on the door of the house. When the door opened, his wife stared at him wide-eyed.

"Juanito!" she called into the house. "Juanito, come quick. Your father has returned."

The handsome young man rushed to the door and embraced Juan. The reunion was tearful and joyous. When his wife started to prepare breakfast, Juan remembered the empanada. He took it out of his backpack and apologized.

"I promised my boss that I would save this to share with you. I'm sorry it's nearly two weeks old and stale."

He cut it open, and to their surprise out spilled 20,000 reales.

J21.5. "Do not leave the highway": counsel proved wise by experience. Robbers encountered.

J21.5.2. "Take side road rather than main one where three roads meet": counsel proved wise by experience.

J21.2. "Do not act when angry": counsel proved wise by experience. Man returns home and sees someone sleeping with his wife. Though he thinks it is a paramour, he restrains himself and finds that it is a newborn son.

One Spanish version has the advice: "If you come to a shortcut, leave the main road." Juan does so and finds that travellers who took the main road were beaten and robbed, while he remained safe on the shortcut. In the same story, a third piece of advice is: "Keep your mouth shut in things that don't concern you."

In the Gesta Romanorum story "The Three Maxims", a merchant sells three maxims to the emperor for a thousand florins with a money-back guarantee.

"The first, my lord, is this: 'Whatever you do, do wisely; and think of the consequences.' The second is: 'Never leave the highway for a byway.' And, thirdly: 'Never stay all night as a guest in that house where you find the master an old man and his wife a young woman.'

These three maxims, if you attend to them, will be extremely serviceable."

White Pebble, Black Pebble
India and Elsewhere

A farmer owed a lot of money to an ugly old moneylender, and he was unable to pay it back. He had a beautiful young daughter. The moneylender said, "If you let me marry your daughter, I'll forgive the debt."

The farmer said No, and his daughter said No.

The moneylender said, "Then we'll let the gods decide. I'll put a white pebble and a black pebble into this bag, and let the girl put her hand in the bag and pick out one without looking. If she picks the white pebble, I will forgive the debt, and she won't have to marry me. If she picks the black pebble, I will forgive the debt and we will be married."

Seeing their hesitation, he added, "And if she refuses, I will take you to court and you will go to jail for defaulting on the debt."

He bent down to pick up two pebbles off the path and put them in the bag. The girl was watching closely, and she noticed that both pebbles were black. He held the bag out to her. She put her hand in and pulled out a pebble, but her hand caught on the mouth of the bag, and she dropped it in such a way that she could pretend she didn't see which one it was before it joined the other pebbles on the path.

"Oh, I'm so sorry for my clumsiness," she said. "I was nervous. But you can look at the remaining pebble, and that way you will know which one I picked."

The moneylender didn't bother looking, because he knew he had been outsmarted. Perhaps he also suspected that being married to such a clever woman might not be to his advantage.

Who Owns the Bag of Silver?
Tibet

An old, blind woodcutter and his son lived on the side of a mountain. One day, as the young man was returning home with a load of wood he found a leather bag on the path containing ten pieces of silver weighing ten ounces each. It was worth a lot of money to anyone, but for him and his father it was a fortune. He showed it to his father and said, "This will support us for the rest of our lives in luxury."

"No," said the old man. "It doesn't belong to us. Take it to the village clerk so he can find the rightful owner. But first let me feel the silver pieces."

He took the ten silver lumps out of the bag and counted them and put them back. The son took the bag into the village and explained to the clerk how he had found it and that his father told him to bring it in. The clerk made a note of it but gave the bag back to the young man, because he didn't want to be responsible for it. A few days later, a merchant came to the clerk's office to report that he had lost a bag of silver. The clerk said he thought he might be able to find it and sent for the young man, asking him to bring in the bag.

The merchant was delighted when he saw it, but it occurred to him that he might be able to make a profit. When he opened the bag and counted the ten pieces of silver, he said to the clerk, "There were twenty pieces of silver in the bag. This young man must have stolen ten of them."

The clerk took one of his employees aside and said to him, "Go to the old woodcutter and ask him what his story is." The employee returned and reported that what the old man told him was the same as his son's story.

The clerk said to the merchant, "I'm sorry, but since this bag has ten pieces of silver and yours had twenty, this one is obviously not yours, so I'll let the young man keep it."

(Adapted from *Tibetan Folk Tales*, by A. L. Shelton, 1925.)

J1172.1. Not the same purse as was lost.

Titanic Thompson
United States

Alvin Clarence Thomas (1892-1974) was an audacious and imaginative gambler and all-round hustler better known as Titanic Thompson: "Titanic" because he sank everyone; "Thompson" because of a newspaper misprint. He specialised in proposition bets – "I bet you I can ..." – and then he'd do it, often with a bit of prior jiggery-pokery. For example, playing high-stakes golf with a steel-core ball after inserting a magnet in the cup. That's fraud, but one of his most famous exploits comes reasonably close to qualifying as a trick, if only because it's a kid versus an adult.

He was eleven years old, fishing in a pool in Arkansas, where he grew up. A man offered to trade his expensive fishing tackle for the boy's water spaniel. Titanic refused to trade, but he made a proposition.

"I'll bet my dog against your tackle that I can mark a stone and throw it in the pool, and the dog will retrieve it."

The man accepted. Titanic drew an X on a stone and threw it in the water. The dog jumped in and returned with what appeared to be the same marked stone. The man handed over the fishing tackle. The trick was that the boy had previously marked every stone in the pool with an X.

Dumb Kid
United States

A barber was cutting a customer's hair when a young boy walked into the shop.

"This is the stupidest kid in the world," the barber whispered to the customer. "Watch this."

207

The barber took a dollar and a quarter out of his pocket and held the dollar in one hand and the quarter in the other and said to the boy, "Which one of these do you want, kid?"

"I'll take the quarter, sir."

The barber gave him the quarter.

"Thank you, sir," the boy said and left the shop.

"See what I mean?" said the barber. "This happens a couple times a week, and he always picks the quarter. The dumb kid never learns."

Haircut finished, the man walked out of the shop and down the street and met the boy coming out of a shop licking an ice cream cone.

"Hey, there, son. I have a question for you. The barber tells me you go through this game a couple times a week and you always choose the quarter. How come you never pick the dollar?"

"'Cause the first time I pick the dollar the game's over."

Miracle as a Trick of God
Hungary

Saint Elizabeth of Hungary (1207-1231), daughter of King Andrew II, is the patron of bakers and beggars. As a child, she would sneak dinner leftovers to the beggars at the gate of the palace. This was forbidden by her father. One cold winter day on her way to the gate with a basket of food, she encountered the king.

"What do you have in the basket?" he asked suspiciously.

"Roses," she said, perhaps forgetting that Hungarian winters are not conducive to the survival of flowers.

But the king had not forgotten.

"Show me," he ordered.

She uncovered the basket to find that the food had suddenly turned into roses.

(Source: *A History of Hungarian Literature*, Frederick Riedl, 1906.)

The One That Got Away (With It)

An election was coming up for a seat on the city council. Neither the incumbent nor the challenger had a clean reputation, but both were popular, the challenger perhaps a bit more so. The operator of an illegal poker game was asked if the results would affect his business. "It depends on who wins," he said.

The incumbent was at an illegal cockfight when he saw the challenger come in. The incumbent left and called the police, who swooped and arrested the challenger and others. (The sergeant explained in his report that they didn't catch all the participants because "some of the inmates escaped by jumping out the window.")

The full story, including who had informed the police, spread quickly in the small city, and the trick probably helped the incumbent to win. But wasn't he just as guilty as the challenger? Yes, but when you have a choice between two crooks you pick the shrewder.

By the way, the poker game continued.

He Was a Stranger
United States

It was the custom for a group of men to sit around the general store chewing the fat with the owner, a committed Christian who knew the Bible inside-out and prided himself on his ability to apply a passage from Holy Writ to any situation.

For example, when a girl came into the store and didn't have enough money to buy some candy, the owner handed her a bagful and quoted, "Suffer the little children to come unto me." Another time, a boy wanted to buy a present for his father but was short of the price on the label. The owner gave him a discount and quoted, "Honour thy father and thy mother."

One day a Cadillac pulled up in front of the store bearing an out-of-state licence plate and towing an expensive horse trailer. A man got out of the car and came into the store and said to the owner, "I need a horse blanket."

The owner went into the stock room and came out with a box. He opened it and said, "Here's a nice one – only $17.75."

Without even glancing at the blanket, the stranger went red in the face and said, "Did you see that Cadillac I drove up in?"

"Yes, sir."

"Do you think a man who drives a Cadillac would settle for a $17.75 horse blanket?"

"I see your point, sir. I'll get another one."

He took the box back to the stock room and came out with another one and opened it. It was obvious to the local men that the blanket was the same brand and grade but a different colour.

"How do you like this one, sir? Much better quality. Only $67.75."

The stranger turned a deeper red.

"Did you notice that brand-new horse trailer I'm hauling?"

"Yes, sir."

"That trailer cost me $100,000, and in that trailer is a Standardbred filly by Muscle Hill that I just bought out of the sales for $350,000, and you offer to sell me a horse blanket that costs only $67.75?"

"I understand completely, sir. Just a moment."

He returned to the stock room and came out with a box and opened it. The men could see that the blanket was the first one he had shown to the stranger, which the stranger hadn't even glanced at.

"Here you are, sir. I think this is what you were looking for. Top of the range, finest quality. Last one in stock. It's yours for $499.99."

"That's more like it," said the man, and he handed over five hundred-dollar bills. They all watched him carry the box out to the Cadillac, and then the men turned to the store owner, to see what Bible reference he would come up with to suit this occasion.

He shrugged and not-quite quoted Matthew 25:35: "He was a stranger, and I took him in."

Mississippi comedian Jerry Clower (1926-1998) told this yarn and may be the original source, but it is widespread among American storytellers.

A Bag of Irish Tricks

The Rebel and the Sergeant

Frank O'Connor fought as a member of the Irish Republican Army (IRA) in the Irish War of Independence (1919-1921). His best-known short story, "Guests of the Nation" (1931), is set during the War. Members of the IRA are holding two captured English soldiers, and over the course of a few days have become friendly with their prisoners. They are shocked when their leader tells them that the Englishmen are really hostages, to be killed if the British execute Irish prisoners. The Irish prisoners are executed, and the Englishmen are killed in retaliation. The story is grimly realistic.

Brendan Behan's 1958 play *The Hostage* echoes that situation, but when an IRA man is executed, the British soldier held hostage is killed in the cross-fire when gardaí raid the house. Behan was a one-time member of the IRA. The 1992 film *The Crying Game* begins with a similar setting before it goes off in another direction.

The basic theme in those fictional works – political animosity mitigated by personal goodwill – has long been a part of Irish consciousness, so the following true story has a special resonance.

During the War, a group of IRA rebels captured a British army sergeant, holding him against a British threat to an IRA man. One of the IRA guards got friendly with the sergeant. When the British threat over their IRA captive was lifted, some of the rebels wanted to kill the sergeant regardless, but the guard who had become friendly with the sergeant prevented the murder, and the sergeant was released unharmed.

The British army from time to time cordoned off a street at random and herded everyone through a check point, where they were searched to see if they were carrying weapons. Anyone discovered to be armed could be shot immediately as a combatant. The IRA man who

212

had befriended the sergeant found himself trapped in one of these operations. He had a handgun with him. The soldiers were watching closely, and he had no way to get rid of the gun without being seen.

As he drew closer to the check point, he saw that one of the soldiers was that same sergeant whose life he had saved. The sergeant recognized him and reckoned he was probably armed. He strode aggressively toward the rebel, grabbed him roughly and threw him through the check point without a search, giving him a parting kick for the sake of appearances and shouting, "You're just a piece of scum." And so saved his life.

(Source T. J. M. Sheehy)

Twisting the Hay-rope

I turned in to the house
Of my love and my hope,
Turned out by her 'oul one
By twisting the rope.
(paraphrasing Red Hanrahan)

It would be some two hundred years ago now that there lived a schoolmaster from Connacht turned itinerant poet named Tomás Ó hAnnracháin, better known as Red Hanrahan. He was itinerant for a good reason: a sweet-talker and serial seducer and all-round trouble-maker, he had been hounded from one community to another, in spite of a talent for singing and dancing and composing poems.

Hanrahan happened to be walking along a road in Munster one day when he heard fiddle music coming from a cottage and invited himself to join the party. The man of the house welcomed him, knowing of his reputation as an entertainer, but his wife, Maurya, familiar with the dark rumours that preceded him wherever he went, objected:

"He has no good name now among the priests, or with women that mind themselves." (Yeats)

213

"They say that there is no place that he'll go to that the women don't love him and that the men don't hate him." (Gregory)

Her objections overruled, Maurya consulted with a neighbour, Sheela, because once Hanrahan laid his eyes on Oona, the beautiful daughter of the house, she knew it would not be easy to dislodge him. It was deemed a grave insult to eject a poet from a house. In Irish tradition, poets have the ability to lay a curse on those who obstruct or displease them, and bad luck, disease and even death can result.

"He has a curse that would split the trees and that would burst the stones. They say the seed will rot in the ground and the milk go from the cows when a poet like him makes a curse, if a person routed him out of the house." (Gregory)

As Hanrahan plied the naive Oona with fair words and flattery, and monopolised her attention by not allowing anyone, including her fiancé, to speak or dance with her, Sheela came up with a plan: "We will put him to twist a hay-rope till he is outside, and then we will shut the door on him."

A rope is made by braiding together fibres like the plaiting of hair. The fibres would often be strands of hay or straw in the old days, and even grass will suffice in an emergency. One person holds the beginning end of the rope and walks backwards as it lengthens, while he gives it a twist in time with the other person's plaiting and splicing of wisps of hay into the rope.

The women told Hanrahan that a wind had come up, and the haycock needed to be tied down, and they didn't have any rope. With a bit of praise for his nimble fingers and general superiority of knowledge, they were able to persuade Hanrahan to twist a hay-rope for them: "I'll hold the hay now, and you'll go twisting it," said Sheela.

Conscious of Oona's eyes on him, Hanrahan concentrated on his craft to show off his expertise and strength, not noticing that he was being subtly guided toward the door as he walked backwards. Once he was

214

outside, the women slammed the door on him and ignored his shouts and curses, which were ineffective because they were not deserved, since he was at least technically not routed out of the house.

This is my retelling of a story which William Butler Yeats based on a folk song and published as "The Twisting of the Rope" in *Stories of Red Hanrahan* in 1897. In 1901, Douglas Hyde (An Craoibhín) made a one-act play in Irish from it, *Casadh an tSúgáin*, which Lady Gregory translated with the title *The Twisting of the Rope*. It was the first play in the Irish language produced in Ireland, with Hyde taking the role of Red Hanrahan to great acclaim. Dr Hyde (1860-1949) was a scholar and a collector of folk songs and tales before he became the first president of an independent Ireland in 1938. Several versions of the song "Casadh an tSúgáin" (in Irish), and the lyrics in Irish and English, can be found on the internet.

The Devil in the Dance Hall
Tooreen, County Mayo, 1954

I'd know it in the sunshine in the rain or in the wind,
I'd know it were I blindfolded with never a guide at all,
I'd know it in the darkness were I deaf and dumb and blind,
The road that leads to Tooreen and Ireland's finest hall.

St. Mary's Hall, Tooreen (Ballyhaunis), dancing 9-3
(ad in *The Western People*, 1952)

But is the devil so foolish as to neglect a grand opportunity on the lonely roads and the small hours for reaping his harvest of souls?

215

(letter to the editor, *The Western People*, 1951, regarding late-night dances)

When I first arrived in Ireland in 1978, hitching around the country for a month, I heard a story from several people that they said happened "about twenty years ago".

There was a dance hall in the tiny village of Tooreen run by the local priest, Father James Horan. Later, as Monsignor Horan, he championed the much-derided nearby "airport in a bog" that opened in 1985 to become the successful Horan International Airport, now the Ireland West Airport Knock. Knock is a pilgrimage site where apparitions of the Blessed Virgin and other saints were reported in 1879. The airport is the fourth busiest in Ireland.

Father Horan's dances were hugely popular, drawing people from as far away as Belfast. I was told that men would cycle 25 miles to the dance after a full day's work and cycle home in the early hours for another day's work. Most of the attendees were regulars and familiar enough to the others that a stranger stood out. This was especially true of a handsome, well-dressed man who entered one night. The young women gazed on him with approval, but when he approached to ask them to dance they suddenly felt a mysterious revulsion.

Eventually, a young woman accepted his invitation, and he whirled her around the dance floor with expertise. After a few dances, he suggested they go outside "for a breath of fresh air", which as everyone knows is code for hugging and smooching. She agreed.

The usual band of young fellows were hanging around outside near the entrance. They reported that the man and the woman got into a big black fancy car parked at the side of the road. After a few minutes, they heard the woman's voice cry out, "Get your filthy paws off me, you dirty devil."

The car disappeared in a puff of smoke, leaving the woman sitting on the ground. A fiery-horned goat wearing clothes ran off down the road. The young fellows shouted

216

into the dance hall, "It's the devil. Come out and look." People rushed out and saw the goat and listened to the whole episode as recounted by the witnesses.

For years after I heard the story, I asked people in Mayo and various storytellers for details or confirmation without success, and as time went by fewer admitted even being aware of it. In 2005, by pure chance I came across an exhibition in Dublin by photographer Éilís Murphy, who grew up near Tooreen. It consisted of photos of the derelict dance hall – and *the true story* about the devil's appearance.

In common with many well-run dances, no alcoholic drinks were served in the Tooreen Dance Hall, and no one "with drink taken" – that is, already drunk – was allowed in. This was the case with those young lads hanging around outside the dance hall on the night of 3 October 1954. Annoyed at being refused admittance, they had concocted a tall tale, stolen a goat, borrowed clothes off a clothesline, dressed the goat, tied flashlights to his horns, and raised the alarm, before sending the goat running down the road. People saw a goat wearing clothes, and, believing their eyes, accepted the lads' instant legend without question.

This was obviously a prank or a hoax, but I believe the fact that it became embedded in the culture as a folk tale elevates it to the status of trick.

(The *Western People* quotes are from Éilís's exhibition.)

Cost-cutting

A gas pipeline was constructed from Cork to Dublin in 1982, crossing 587 land holdings. A farmer whose property was being dug up approached a worker and asked how much he would charge to run a line from his house to the pipe. Fifty pounds was the answer. The farmer paid gladly, envisioning a lifetime of free gas. The worker said he would inform the farmer when the connection was made. A few weeks later, the worker came and installed a line from the farmer's cooker to some distance from the house. After a month, the gas stopped flowing. The worker had moved on with the pipeline, so the farmer unearthed the line running into his house and followed it to an empty gas bottle – worth £5 full – hidden in a clump of bushes.

Three competing gas companies in 19th-century Dublin were rumoured to be not above such trickery themselves. It was said that some workers were paid a bonus to surreptitiously connect their company's customers to another company's pipe.

Trinity College

John Engle reports in *Trinity Student Pranks* that in 1747 a student was arrested by a bailiff for non-payment of bills and put in jail. His fellow students grabbed the bailiff and held his head under the communal water pump at the college, a popular form of punishment.

A story I heard long ago tells that a teaching fellow of the college had got behind in his rent and was arrested by a bailiff and jailed. After he was released, one day he noticed the same bailiff strolling into the college. He pointed him out to a group of students and told them that the bailiff had been responsible for his incarceration.

"I'm sure," he said to them with possibly a wink, "that you gentlemen would never be so cruel as to nail that man's ears to the water pump."

They did, of course, and that bailiff was never seen on the campus again.

A Hare Coursing Stroke

In Ireland, a particularly imaginative trick is called a stroke, and a major stroke is called a coup.

The controversial blood sport of hare coursing, illegal in the UK since 2005, seems close to being banned in Ireland. Hares are valued for their ability to elude the hounds. While the greyhounds or lurchers (a cross between a sight-hound and a non-sight-hound) are muzzled in Ireland, it has been reported that hares are sometimes killed.

There was a hare that was famous for never being caught. He always escaped though a gap in the hedge. One day, an old man arrived at the course betting that his lurcher could catch that hare. A glance at the hound suggested to the experts that they were on to a good thing, and they parted gladly with their stakes.

The hare was let loose, and after a fair start the lurcher was slipped. The hare turned and dodged, eluding the hound, and finally bolted for the gap in the hedge with the hound close on his heels. To the amazement of the experts and the gratification of the lurcher's owner, the hound came prancing up to them with the hare in its mouth.

The old man collected his winnings and waited until everyone had left, then he went to the gap in the hedge and removed the car windscreen he had placed there earlier.

Toss Byrne's Stroke

Thomas "Toss" Byrne owned the popular Fountain Pub in Avoca, County Wicklow, now renowned as Fitzgeralds in the 1996-2001 TV series *Ballykissangel*. He announced one day that he was going to sell up and move with his family to Canada. He sold the pub for a good price, and his friends and neighbours and customers took up a collection to help them on their way. But he only went as far as the Woodenbridge Hotel a few miles down the road, which he bought with the proceeds of the sale of the Fountain. All the good will he had built up at the Fountain,

219

along with many of his former customers, relocated along with him. Then he sold the Woodenbridge and bought the pub on the N11 near Gorey in County Wexford still called "Toss Byrne's".

A Rathnew Stroke

A poor widow living in a cottage in Rathnew, County Wicklow, fell into arrears in her rent, and after several warnings the bailiffs arrived to evict her. As soon as they had moved all her furniture into the front garden, she suddenly produced the full of the back rent.

"Why didn't you pay the rent before we went to all the trouble of moving this furniture out?" they asked in amazement.

"Never mind that," she said. "Ye can go now and have your lunch, and then come back and put all the furniture back where it was."

They went away, and while they were gone the widow gave the cottage the first thorough cleaning it had had in years, which of course was the reason she wanted the furniture temporarily removed at no cost to herself.

Bosco's Stroke

Bosco had a photographic memory and a glib tongue. Having read a book on horticulture, he convinced a doctor that he was an authority on roses, and the doctor hired him to turn the extensive grounds around his large house into a spectacle of colour. Bosco paid some men from the labour exchange to dig sixty holes, while he personally organized the acquisition of the plants. In due course, sixty burlap-wrapped bundles with thorny stems sticking out were deposited in the holes, and the doctor paid Bosco the agreed £600.

It was autumn, and since one bunch of thorny stems looks much like another, the doctor had no reason to be suspicious throughout the winter. But the Spring revealed all, when he discovered that he was raising the largest crop of blackberries in Belfast.

The doctor confronted Bosco with the evidence and made him remove the bramble bushes. Bosco offered to return the £600, but the doctor refused, saying that he had been taken in fair and square. Not only that, he hired Bosco as his permanent gardener, but with one stipulation: that he would not plant any rose bushes.

(Source: the late Hughie McCusker of Rathfriland, County Down, who was my neighbour in Avoca, County Wicklow, and a friend of Bosco.)

Spading the Garden

Dublin's favourite folk singer and raconteur, the late Ronnie Drew (1934-2008), told the following story as factual. Stephen Behan, father of the playwright Brendan, was a house painter. His wife, Kathleen – "mother of all the Behans" – was the sister of Peadar Kearney, author of the lyrics to "The Soldier's Song", the triumphal and militaristic Irish national anthem. The whole family was extremely nationalistic. Brendan joined the IRA at the age of 16 and was imprisoned for possession of explosives and for the attempted murder of two gardaí.

On the many days that Stephen was without a job to do, he left the house anyway in his painting clothes with his buckets and brushes and ladder and spent the day in the pub. Kathleen wanted to plant flowers in the spacious front garden of their house in Crumlin. She ordered a load of manure and asked Stephen to turn it under. He complained about "the waste of good drinking money on horseshit" and kept putting her off, saying he was too busy or too tired.

Eventually, tired of her nagging, Stephen phoned the Special Branch of the gardaí anonymously and told them that Stephen Behan had been seen burying guns for the IRA in his front garden. The gardaí were very familiar with the Behan family's reputation and went immediately to the house and dug up the garden. When they had finished with the spadework, having found no weapons, Kathleen planted her flowers.

H588.7. Father's counsel: find treasure within a foot of the ground. (Sons dig everywhere and thus loosen soil of vineyard, which becomes fruitful.)

How to Quit a Job

At the age of 21, Ronnie Drew landed a position as a night telephonist with the Posts and Telegraphs: a secure job for life with a pension at the end. It was soul-destroying work for an ambitious and imaginative person, and before the end of a year he was thinking of quitting. Then an incident occurred that took the decision out of his hands.

A woman dialled "10" and Ronnie took the call. "I knew by the sound of her that she was a bombastic oul' bitch," Ronnie recalled in his autobiography. She wanted to be put through to London. He told her that there was a queue and it could take an hour and a half. She insisted that the call was urgent. Ronnie explained that only a government minister could jump the queue, "and would she ever go and fuck off and not be annoying me."

"Young man, do you realize to whom you are speaking?"

"No, madam."

"I am the wife of the Minister for Posts and Telegraphs, and I will complain most severely about your attitude and your behaviour."

"Do you realize, madam, to whom you are speaking?"

"I certainly do not."

"Thanks be to Jaysus," said Ronnie, and he pulled the plug.

Management found out anyway, and he was invited to resign.

(Both of the above stories were in Ronnie's performance repertoire and appear in his autobiography, *Ronnie*, Penguin Ireland, 2008.)

The Disappearing Parking Ticket Book

It sounds like an urban legend, but this story was circulating in 1980s Dublin as factual.

An enterprising young boy approached a motorist who had just received a parking ticket and offered to settle the problem for a small cash payment. The motorist paid. The boy ran after the traffic warden and snatched his ticket book and threw it into the River Liffey, which meant that there was no record of the ticket.

The Train in the Tunnel

An Irishman and an English soldier sat facing a beautiful young woman and her mother on a train many years ago. There were no lights on the train, so when it went into a tunnel, it was completely dark. There was the sound of a kiss and then a loud slap. When the train came out of the tunnel, the soldier was holding his hand to his cheek, the mother glanced fondly at her daughter, the daughter's face was blank, and the Irishman was the picture of innocence.

The soldier thought, "The Irishman must have kissed the girl, and she tried to slap him and hit me instead."

The mother thought, "My daughter is a good girl. The soldier kissed her and she slapped him."

The daughter thought, "The soldier must be gay and kissed the Irishman and got slapped for it."

The Irishman thought, "Ireland one, England zero. The next time we go into a tunnel I'll smooch my hand again and give the soldier another slap."

A Trick Backfires

Irish journalist John McEntee admitted to a failed trick in his memoir *I'm Not One to Gossip, But ....* He was anxious to have a good view of Pope John Paul II conducting Mass during his visit to the Marian shrine at Knock, County Mayo, in 1979. He organized a wheelchair, a lap rug and a chauffeur with a local man in a meeting over four pints of Guinness each. The trick worked, and he had a ringside seat. The problem was that the Pope was two hours late, and McEntee's concentration was diverted by all that Guinness trying to find a way out.

Racing

Horse racing is a more widely popular sport in Britain and Ireland than in most other countries, appealing to all classes. The first two stories were the stuff of not only dreams but also of prominent newspaper articles at the time they occurred, and they are still remembered by the general public, partly because they are frequently recycled on television.

Murphy's Stroke: The Gay Future Affair
Britain
26 August 1974

On 12 March 1975, Irishman Tony Murphy and his accomplices were charged with "conspiring with others to defraud bookmakers by attempting to win by means of fraud and ill-practice multi and single wagers made by them or on their behalf on Gay Future, Ankerwyke and Opera Cloak" at Cartmel race course in England the previous year. Asked during the trial whether he felt his plot was a criminal act or a stroke of genius, Murphy replied, "A stroke of genius, sir."

Murphy and one of his confederates were found guilty of fraud, though the sympathetic judge told Murphy afterwards, "It would be absurd to classify you as a fraudulent man."

"Sure, I planned the whole thing," Murphy admitted. "Why not? It's every man's dream, isn't it, to skin the bookies?"

A stroke it may have been, but it was clearly a criminal act, and it only appears here as a prelude to Barney Curley's Yellow Sam Coup the following year, which severely inconvenienced the bookies but was not illegal. Both schemes were complex, with some similarities in their tactics. This is a simplified summary of how the Gay Future Affair was carried out.

Murphy and others formed a syndicate to buy the capable chestnut Gay Future, who had never raced in Britain, and a ringer – a lookalike chestnut – a poor horse who would run in Britain under the name of Gay Future and build a reputation as a loser. The horses were switched two days before the race at Cartmel, a third-rate course known for poor quality races. It was a bank holiday weekend, one of the busiest in the racing calendar, and the professional gamblers and bookmakers would be concentrating on the higher-quality races elsewhere.

The syndicate and their confederates went to a large number of betting shops in Ireland and Britain and placed small bets on Gay Future, as well as combination bets on him and two horses entered at Plumpton and Southwell, Ankerwyke and Opera Cloak, who were never meant to run. When the two decoys were withdrawn late on the excuse that their horse boxes had broken down on the way to the race courses, the bets rolled over on to Gay Future, who won at 10-1.

However, some of the bookies smelled a rat and informed the police. It was soon discovered that the two withdrawn decoys had never left their stables, and a full investigation was begun. In the end, the Irish and some British bookies paid up, but the scheme, which would have returned some £300,000 if it hadn't been rumbled, made a profit of only £10,000.

Barney Curley: The Yellow Sam Coup
Bellewstown, County Meath, Ireland
26 June 1975

"It was there to be done – and it worked."

Barney Curley, notorious gambler, failed bookmaker and mediocre trainer of run-of-the-mill horses, came up with an audacious plan to dupe the bookies. He bought a cheap horse that he called Yellow Sam, his father's nickname. Sam jumped well over hurdles but performed badly in certain ground conditions, so Curley ran the horse against his betters on unfavourable ground to establish a poor form. Then he entered him in a low-grade amateur hurdle race at Bellewstown, a minor track known for the low quality of racing, when ground conditions were favourable for Sam and unfavourable for the competition. The odds-makers missed telltale signs in the horse's form, and he was priced at 20-1.

Down to his last £15,000, Barney put the full amount on the horse. However, as a well-known gambler who had a knack of winning, he couldn't be seen to be betting on the horse, or else the price would fall dramatically. So he hired a small army of confederates to place moderate bets at 150 shops around Ireland and tied up the only public phone on the race course for 25 minutes before the start of the race, so off-course bookies couldn't warn their on-course colleagues of a suspected coup in the making and bring the price down. The Gay Future conspirators used the same tactic.

Yellow Sam won at 20-1, netting Barney £300,000 – about €2 million in today's money. The bookies were furious, but it was all perfectly legal, and they had to stump up. It was reported that they paid in £1 notes wadded up and stuffed in 108 sacks.

Barney tells the full story in his autobiography *Giving a Little Back* (1998), the proceeds of which go to Direct Aid for Africa. "It's the safest bet there is," he says in the book. "Give Him one good work, and He'll always give you back ten."

Barney Curley (Perhaps) Strikes Again

On 22 January 2014, a four-horse gamble cost the bookies more than £2 million, to count only the winnings that went to the organizers of the coup. As the odds tumbled from overnight or morning prices, eagle-eyed punters took full advantage. All four horses had some connection to Barney Curley.

Bookmakers Coral said: "Once the name Barney Curley was put into the mix – although there is no official confirmation he was involved – there is no question a lot of the bets placed would have been from punters with no knowledge of any plot but who were simply joining in the gamble." Paddy Power: "This is a weapons grade coup, they've well and truly taken our pants down. I'm only jealous I wasn't on myself!" BetVictor: "just another well-planned and, it would appear, well-executed gamble involving four horses with a direct connection to Barney Curley".

There is only circumstantial evidence that Curley was *directly* involved.

Seven Summits trained by Curley until 27 April 2013 – overnight price 7-1 – won at 9-4.

Eye of the Tiger trained by Curley until 18 November 2013 – overnight 10-1 – won at evens.

Indus Valley, same trainer as Eye of the Tiger – 7-1 overnight (20-1 morning with one bookie) – won at 9-4.

Low Key trained by a former assistant of Curley – 7-1 morning – won at 4-7.

On the following day, Pipers Piping was evens favourite – in from 20-1 – for the 5.00 at Kempton until shortly before the off. He hadn't won a race for nearly two years, since February 2012, hadn't run since February 2013, and had lost his previous twelve races by up to 76 lengths. Why the short price? Another coup was expected. The owner until two days previously was John Butler, the trainer of Low Key. Pipers Piping went off the 6-4 favourite and came in a respectable 7th of 13 runners, only four lengths behind the 16-1 winner, Prohibition, who was owned by John Butler until two days previously and hadn't won since March 2012. Curiously, the stewards called in the trainers and jockeys of Pipers Piping, Prohibition and second favourite Tijuca (who finished last) *before* the race for a discussion.

Getting the Lead Out

There are many ways of enhancing the probability of a horse winning or losing a race. Winning is supposedly what racing is all about, although not necessarily *every* race. Most methods of "holding" a horse – preventing it from running at its full potential – are illegal because they cheat the bettor and can harm the horse's health if drugs are used; others sail a bit close to the wind and their legality is arguable. This is one of those.

In a claiming race, any horse can be bought at the claim price. You enter a horse in a $5000 claiming race, and it can be claimed by another trainer for $5000. This is to ensure that horses of the same class compete against one another. The horse you paid $20,000 for will stand a better chance of winning, but if it's claimed you get only $5000 plus any prize money; you lose at least $10,000. You enter your claim on a form and put it into a sealed box before the race. No one knows you have claimed the horse. As soon as the race is finished, the box is opened and you collect the horse on the track in full public view. The previous owner and trainer have no contact with the horse. If the horse won, the previous owner gets the purse. If it died or was seriously injured during the race, you have bought a half-ton of dog food.

A trainer had been watching a horse run by another stable. The horse had breeding and conformation and ran well but always faded several lengths before the finish line. The trainer was puzzled at this but took a chance and bought the horse out of a claiming race. Before you buy a horse in the usual way, you have your vet and farrier (blacksmith) check it over. The first thing you do when you claim a horse is call your vet and farrier for an inspection.

The farrier found lead plates under the horse's shoes. The buying trainer reckoned that each lead plate was holding the horse back at least a length in a six-furlong race. The previous trainer was a gambler. He was obviously "holding" the horse for several races to build up

the odds, after which he would remove the lead, put a
hefty wager on the horse and let it win at a good price.

Racing Shorts

Back in the days before televised races, a man living
above a bookies shop cut the phone line that carried the
results to the bookies and diverted it into a tape recorder.
He listened to the results as he recorded them, went down
to the shop and placed his bet on the winner, then returned
to his flat and played the tape on the phone line into the
bookies. Greed got the better of his judgement, and he was
caught when he extended his uncanny winning streak too
far.

As a freelance groom at a race track in the United
States, I took a horse to the paddock on a day when it was
raining so heavily you couldn't see more than a few horse
lengths. That meant, of course, that the race was invisible
to the stewards and their cameras. My trainer's jockey
lodged an objection following the race. He accused
another jockey of holding his horse's saddle towel,
thereby slowing down his horse while giving the offending
jockey's horse an advantage. The offending jockey
admitted to the stewards that he had held the saddle towel,
but he said he had noticed the saddle was slipping, and he
was only trying to help.

A bookie owned a useless horse. He entered it in a race
that had only two other runners in order to pick up a bit of
place money, and he offered an attractive price on it to
entice chancers. An old man came along and placed a
substantial bet on the nag, which, to the bookie's surprise,
won handily.
When the man collected his winnings, the bookie said,
"I own that horse, and on form it had no chance of
winning. Why did you back it?"
"I own the other two."

Pranks

This is a variant of the old Irish custom of sending the fool further. A Japanese car salesman was demonstrating his company's latest product at a motor show in Dublin. It was a talking car, the kind that politely orders you to shut your door and fasten your seatbelt – in English, of course. An Irishman solemnly informed the salesman that Ireland is a bilingual country, and so the car could not be sold here legally unless it also spoke the first official language: Irish. The salesman phoned headquarters in a panic, but apparently the matter was sorted out eventually. Have you ever heard a Japanese car speak Irish?

John Engle (*Trinity Student Pranks*) relates stories of the rivalry between the Philosophical Society (the Phil) and the Historical Society (the Hist) at Trinity College in Dublin, in which the Phil frequently steals the Hist's revered treasure, an antique wooden ballot box used as a podium for their meetings. One time the Phil wrapped it as a Christmas present and placed it beneath the Christmas tree in the Hist common room. The Hist searched high and low in all the wrong places and threatened to report the theft to the gardaí (Irish police), so the Phil had to inform them that the box had been in their possession all along.

Two young women saw the chance for a bit of fun when a clergyman went for a swim, leaving his clerical garb and a camera on the beach. While he was out of sight, they stripped and took turns dressing up in portions of the man's clothing and snapping pictures of each other in provocative poses – with his camera.

As a prank for a dinner party, a well-known Irish food expert once prepared dishes designed to generate a form of natural gas. While circulating among her guests after dinner, she would nip frequently into the back garden to relieve her own internal combustion, and then stroll back in to amuse herself with the painful contortions on the faces of her victims.

The Great Rose Bowl Hoax of 1961 is deservedly described as the "greatest collegiate prank of all time". California Institute of Technology (Caltech) students managed to alter the instructions for the use of Washington Huskies supporters' flip-cards to spell out "CALTECH". The complex details of this ingenious and well-executed stunt are available online.

Bones

"Bones" is the term used by storytellers for the bare outline of a story. They contain the basic elements of the narrative, and it is left to the teller to supply the setting, the description of the characters, and the dialogue. The following bones are examples of some 2500 entries in the Stith-Thompson *Motif-Index of Traditional Folk-Literature* (ST), which can be found in several places on the internet.

You can use the motifs to construct your own versions of these centuries-old tales, but keep in mind that it is a major offence against the spirit of story to change the narrative of a traditional tale. As the 12th-century Book of Leinster scribe says at the end of the Irish epic *Táin Bó Cuailnge* (The Cattle Raid of Cooley): "A blessing be upon all such as shall faithfully keep the Táin in memory as it stands here and shall not add any other form to it."

Some of the stories are very short, not much longer than the ST entry, like this one from *The Kathá Sarit Ságara or Ocean of the Streams of Story* published in 1880, followed by the ST entry condensing that story and another entry referring to a related tale.

"Once on a time a snake came and ate the nestlings of a certain crane, as fast as they were born; that grieved the crane. So, by the advice of a crab, he went and strewed pieces of fish from the dwelling of a mongoose as far as the hole of the snake, and the mongoose came out, and following up the pieces of fish, eating as it went on, was led to the hole of the snake, which it saw and entered, and killed him and his offspring."

K401.1.1. Trail of stolen goods made to lead to dupe. The crane in revenge for the loss of her young ones strews pieces of fish from the dwelling of the mongoose to that of the snake. The mongoose follows the trail and kills the snake.

K401.2.2. Necklace dropped by crow into snake's hole leads men to kill snake which had eaten the crow's fledglings.

J1565.1 Fox and crane invite each other. Fox serves the food on a flat dish so that the crane cannot eat. Crane serves his food in a bottle.

J1612. The lazy ass repaid in kind. Loaded with salt, he falls down in the river and lightens his burden. His master then loads him with sponges so that the next time the ass tries the trick he increases his load.

K334.1. The raven with cheese in his mouth. The fox flatters him into singing, so that he drops the cheese.

K815.6. Snake promises to do no harm to frog. Kills him. (*Panchatantra* III, 13, 368)

K1818.5. Animal feigns lameness. (Kildeer and other birds feign injury to avoid capture.)

K335.1.4. Animals climb on one another's backs and cry out; frighten robbers. (The tale of the Bremen musicians is the best known version of this motif.)

K335.0.4.2. Porcupine, made to believe that rabbit's ears are horns, flees and leaves food behind.

K345.2. Thief sent into well by trickster. A weeping boy tells a passing thief that he has lost a silver cup in a well. The thief takes off his clothes and goes after the cup, intending to keep it. He finds nothing. When he comes up, his clothes have been stolen. (African proverb: "When thief thief thief, God laugh.")

J1216. Wine seller carries water into his cellar. Man [who knows he is watering the drink] raises alarm pretending that he thought the house must be afire.

K1765. Bluff in court: the stone in the purse. A poor man has a stone in his purse to throw at the judge if he is sentenced. The judge thinks that he has money to use as a bribe and acquits him. (This is a Hodja tale.)

K1771.3. Sham threat: something he has never done before. Beggar says, "If you do not give me alms I shall have to do something I have never done before." The alms are given and he is asked what he would have had to do. "Work." (A Hodja tale.)

K341.1. Trickster reports lost money; searchers leave him in possession of premises. Unable to find a place by the inn fire, the trickster mentions that he has lost money on the road. One by one the guests slip out to search and leave him the fire.

K275. Counting out pay. Hole in the hat and hat over a pit. (Also used when the Devil is counting out payment for a person's soul. The Devil gives up.)

K231.13. Agreement to leave sum of money on coffin of friend. One puts on his share in cash; other makes out a check for the total amount and takes cash left by the other.

K185.4.1. Deceptive land purchase: as much land as can be covered by saint's hood. Only by snatching up hood does seller prevent it from covering whole territory. (This is an Irish story about Saint Brigit and her cloak.)

K185.1. Deceptive land purchase: ox-hide measure. As much land bought as can be surrounded by an ox-hide. The hide is cut into very small strips. (Dido used this trick to get land to build Carthage, and Santo Domingo did the same when he founded a hostel for pilgrims in the town named for him, Santo Domingo de la Calzada, on the Camino de Santiago in La Rioja, Spain.)

K2111.2. Spurned woman accuses man of theft. (A story with this motif is set in Santo Domingo de la Calzada.)

K239. Refusal to tell about the Rhine treasure, though condition demanded is fulfilled when the only one who knows where it is is killed.

2412 E. When the "Danes" (Vikings) have been reduced to two, a father and his son, the Irish try to get from them the secret of how they made beer from heather. The father tells them to kill his son, and that he will then tell them the secret. When the son had been put to death, the old Dane then said to his captors: "Put me to death also, if ye so will, for I will never reveal the secret." (Ó Súilleabháin, *The Types of the Irish Folktale*.)

103. A beggarman offers a priest some money which he has stolen from him. The priest, unaware that it is his own money, refuses to accept it, and tells him to give it to the owner. The beggarman replies that he has already done so, but that the owner refused to take it. The priest then advises him to keep it. (Ó Súilleabháin, *A Handbook of Irish Folklore*.)

K112.2. "Soup stone" sold. It needs only the addition of a few vegetables and a bit of meat. (A tramp with little in his pockets but a stone to throw at hostile dogs convinces a person that he can make soup out of the stone and a pot of boiling water. He tastes the water and suggests that salt, pepper, herbs, vegetables, meat, etc. would improve it. Neighbours contribute ingredients. All enjoy the finished product and praise the magic stone. Most storytellers include this tale in their repertoire. William Butler Yeats made it into a play, *The Pot of Broth*, in 1902.)

K1132. Peter receives the blows twice. Peter and Christ are sleeping in the same bed. The drunken host returns and beats Peter, who thereupon changes places with Christ. The host then comes in to beat the other lodger and beats Peter again. (Iceland, Lithuania, Africa)

Sources

Álvarez Blázquez, Xosé Ma., version, introduction and notes, *O Ciprianillo: Os Tesouros de Galicia*, Edicións Castrelos, Vigo, 1974.

Aparicio Casado, Buenaventura, *Mouras, Serpientes, Tesoros y Otros Encantos*, Ediciós do Castro, Sada, A Coruña, Galicia, 1999.

Árnason, Jón, *Icelandic Legends*, a selection from his 1862 collection *Icelandic National Stories and Tales*, translated by George E. J. Powell and Eiríkur Magnússon, 1864.

Aventuras: see Meza, *Aventuras*.

Baraga, Frederic, *A Dictionary of the Otchipwe Language*, 1853, 1878. Facsimile online.

Barry, Michael, and Patrick Sammon, *Dublin's Strangest Tales: Extraordinary but True Stories*, Portico, London, 2013.

Bhatta, Somadeva, *The Kathá Sarit Ságara or Ocean of the Streams of Story*, C.H. Tawney, trans., Calcutta, 1880, 1884. Eleventh-century collection of stories from India.

Boccaccio's 14th-century *Decameron*

Borrow, George, trans., *The Turkish Jester; or, The Pleasantries of Cogia Nasr Eddin Effendi*, 1884.

Carleton, William, *Redmond Count O'Hanlon, the Irish Rapparee: An Historical Tale*, (an adventure novel), London, Dublin, 1862.

Clouston, W. A., *Popular Tales and Fictions: Their Migrations and Transformations*, 1887.

Colarusso, John, trans., *Nart Sagas from the Caucasus*, Princeton University Press, 2002.

Colarusso, John, and Tamirlan Salbiev, eds., Walter May, trans., *Tales of the Narts: Ancient Myths and Legends of the Ossetians*, Princeton University Press, 2016.

Cole, Maria Cook, *Philippine Folk Tales*, 1916.

Compton, Margaret, *American Indian Fairy Tales*, 1907. (Schoolcraft's *Myth* retold for children)

237

Coren, Stanley, *Gods, Ghosts, and Black Dogs: the Fascinating Folklore and Mythology of Dogs*, Veloce Publishing, Dorchester, UK, 2016.

Cosgrave, John, *A Genuine History of the Lives and Actions of the Most Notorious Irish Highwaymen, Tories and Rapparees*, 1776; first published c. 1747.

Cosgrave, John, *The Surprizing Adventures of Redmond O'Hanlon*, Dublin, various editions with similar titles from about 1823.

Cross, Samuel Hazzard and Olgerd P. Sherbowitz-Wetzor, *The Russian Primary Chronicle: Laurentian Text*, The Mediaeval Academy of America, Cambridge, Massachusetts, 1953.

Curley, Barney, *Giving a Little Back*, HarperCollinsWillow, 1998.

De Trueba, Antonio, *Cuentos Populares*, Brockhaus, Leipzig, 1885.

Dictionary of Irish Biography, Royal Irish Academy / Cambridge University Press, 2009.

Drew, Ronnie, *Ronnie*, Penguin Ireland, 2008.

Du Halde, J. B., *A description of the empire of China and Chinese-Tartary*, 1741 (*Description géographique, historique, chronologique, politique, et physique de l'empire de la Chine et de la Tartarie chinoise*, 1735).

Engle, John, *Trinity Student Pranks: A History of Mischief & Mayhem*, The History Press Ireland, 2013.

Espinosa, Aurelio Macedonio, *Cuentos Populares Españoles*, Stanford University, 1923.

Gesta Romanorum ("Deeds of the Romans"), an early 14th-century collection of international legends and folk tales gathered by monks and used as a resource by authors and preachers.

Girgado, Luis Alonzo, *Cuentos Populares*, Tambre Narrativa, A Coruña, Galicia, Spain, 1993.

Guelbenzu, José María, *Cuentos Populares Españoles*, Vol. II, Ediciones Siruela, Madrid, 1997.

Hale, Leslie, *John Philpot Curran: His Life and Times*, Cape, London, 1958.

Huellas: see Meza, *Huellas*.

Hyde, Douglas, and Lady Gregory, *Casadh an tSúgáin*, An Cló-Chumann, Dublin, 1901.

Kennedy, Patrick, *The Book of Modern Irish Anecdotes: Humour, Wit and Wisdom*, Gill, Dublin, 1872.

Larrañaga, Juan Garmendia, *Mitos y leyendas de los Vascos*, Haranburu Editor, Donostia, 1995.

Laval, Ramón A., *Cuentos de Pedro Urdemales*, Imprenta Cervantes, Santiago de Chile, 1925.

Leo the Deacon; see Talbot.

Lutz, Deborah, *The Brontë Cabinet: Three Lives in Nine Objects*, Norton, 2015.

Malcolm, John, *Sketches of Persia*, John Murray, London, 1861.

Mathers, E. Powys, trans., *The Book of the Thousand Nights and One Night*, from the French translation by J. C. Mardrus, 1923.

McArdle, Joseph, *Irish Legal Anecdotes*, Gill & Macmillan, Dublin, 1995.

McEntee, John, *I'm Not One to Gossip, But ...*, Biteback Publishing, London, 2016.

Merrell, Floyd, *Exu: Trickster by Default*, 2003. Online.

Meza, Miguelángel, *Perurima Pypore (Las Huellas de Perurimá – The Footsteps of Perurimá)*, Spanish translation by Maurolugo, Servilobro, Asunción, Paraguay, 2010.

Meza, Miguelángel and Domingo Adolfo Aguilera, *Perurima Rekovekue (Aventuras de Perurimá – Adventures of Perurimá)*, Spanish translation by Carlos Villagra Marsal and Domingo Adolfo Aguilera, Diario Popular, Asunción, Paraguay, 2010.

Munro, Hector H., *The Rise of the Russian Empire*, 1900; source of Leo the Deacon quote.

O'Grady, Standish Hayes, *Silva Gadelica*, William & Norgate, London, 1892. Also online.

Ó hÓgáin, Dáithí, *The Lore of Ireland: An Encyclopaedia of Myth, Legend and Romance*, Collins Press, Wilton, Cork, 2006.

Ó Súilleabháin, Seán, and Reidar Th. Christiansen, *The Types of the Irish Folktale*, in FF Communications, Vol. LXXVII, No. 188, Helsinki, 1968.

Ó Súilleabháin, Seán, *A Handbook of Irish Folklore*, 1942. Also in e-format.

Percy, Bishop Thomas, *Reliques of Ancient English Poetry* (Percy's *Reliques*), 1765.

Petronius, *Satyricon*, first century AD. Translation by W. C. Firebaugh, 1922.

Piñeiro de San Miguel, Esperanza and Andrés Gómez Blanco, *De Lenda en Lenda: Camiños máxicos polo noroeste de Galicia*, Xunta de Galicia, Ferrol, 1999.

Primary Chronicle; see Cross

Riedl, Frederick, *A History of Hungarian Literature*, 1906.

Robinson, Gail and Douglas Hill, *Coyote the Trickster*, Piccolo, London, 1975, 1981.

Rose, Wendy, *Academic Squaw: Reports to the World from the Ivory Tower*; The Blue Cloud Quarterly XXIII:4. 1977; *The Remembered Earth*, 1978; *Pocket Poetry*, November 1978.

Sainero, Ramón, *La Huella Celta en España e Irlanda*, Ediciones Akal, 1998.

Schoolcraft, Henry R., *The Myth of Hiawatha and Other Oral Legends, Mythologic and Allegoric, of the North American Indians*, 1856.

Schoolcraft, Henry R., *The Indian Fairy Book: From the Original Legends*, 1916.

Shah, Tahir (son of Idris Shah), *In Arabian Nights*, Doubleday, 2008.

Shields, Hugh, *Narrative Singing in Ireland: Lays, Ballads, Come-All-Yes and Other Songs*, Irish Academic Press, Newbridge, Kildare, 1993.

Steel, Flora Annie, *Tales of the Punjab*, London & New York: Macmillan and Co., 1894.

Swift, Jonathan, *The Works of the Rev. Jonathan Swift, Volume 1*, Thomas Sheridan, et al., eds., 1784.

Talbot, Alice-Mary and Denis F. Sullivan, trans, *The History of Leo the Deacon. Byzantine Military*

Expansion in the Tenth Century, Dumbarton Oaks Studies XLI, Washington, D.C., 2005.

Tarlton, Richard, *Newes out of Purgatorie*, c. 1590.

Thompson, Stith, *Tales of the North American Indians*, 1929.

Trevelyan, G. M., *A Shortened History of England*, Penguin Books, Harmondsworth, 1980.

Uí Ógáin, Ríonach, *Immortal Dan: Daniel O'Connell in Irish Folk Tradition*, Geography Publications, Dublin, 1995.

Vyas, Chiman L., *Folk Tales of Zambia*, NECZAM (National Education Company of Zambia), Lusaka, 1972, 1974. This edition of the book has been adapted as a reader for secondary school students studying English. Vyas (1917-1973), a journalist and poet from India, was a secondary school teacher and a research officer in the Department of Cultural Services who loved Zambian culture and collected folk tales and songs in the villages, mostly at night because of opposition from the colonial authorities. He was killed in 1973 in a blast during a series of bombings that targeted activists for independence.

White, Horace, trans., *The Roman History of Appian of Alexandria*, (*Historia Romana*, AD 165), 1899.

Yeats, William Butler, *Stories of Red Hanrahan*, Macmillan, New York, 1914.

Online Sources

URLs are not given because they can too often be short-lived.

Mediaeval Tales, Henry Morley, ed. (includes Tales from the Gesta Romanorum)

Gesta Romanorum

Cuentos Populares, Antonio de Trueba

Trickster tales

Stith Thompson *Motif-Index of Traditional Folk-Literature*

Five Eggs – *Revista de Folklore*

Nasruddin Hodja

Stone Soup (also known as Nail Soup)

The Pot of Broth – Yeats

Myth of Hiawatha

Philippines Folk Tales

Seventy Tales of a Parrot

North American Tricksters

Native American Lore (Mount Shasta)

Nart Tales: a variety of text and video material. Start with Amjad Jaimoukha's page.